THE HIDDEN POWER OF RELENTLESS STEWARDSHIP

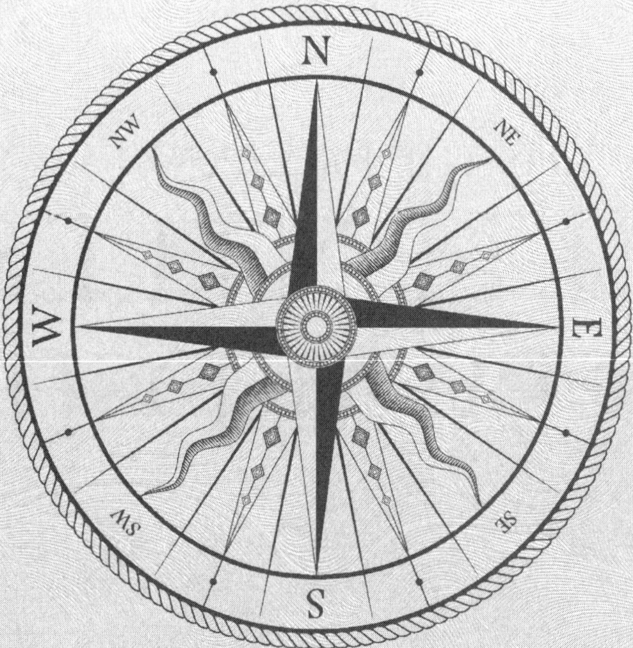

FLORIDA HOSPITAL

Since 1908

THE HIDDEN POWER OF RELENTLESS STEWARDSHIP

5 KEYS *to* DEVELOPING *a* WORLD-CLASS ORGANIZATION

DON JERNIGAN, PHD

with Steve Halliday, PHD

RosettaBooks®

THE HIDDEN POWER OF RELENTLESS STEWARDSHIP

FLORIDA HOSPITAL CREDITS:

EDITOR-IN-CHIEF	Todd Chobotar
INTERNAL PEER REVIEWERS	Karen Tilstra, PhD
	Josef Ghosn, EdD
	Mark Hertling, MA
EXTERNAL PEER REVIEWERS	Shirley Freed, PhD
	Scott Morris, MD
PROMOTION	Caryn McCleskey
PRODUCTION	Lillian Boyd
COPY EDITOR	Pam Nordberg
PHOTOGRAPHY	Spencer Freeman
DESIGN	Hsu + Associates

RosettaBooks editions are available to the trade through Ingram distribution services, ipage.ingramcontent.com or (844) 749-4857. For special orders, catalogues, events, or other information, please write to production@rosettabooks.com.

AUTHOR'S NOTE

This book contains many stories. In order to preserve the privacy of some of those involved, I have disguised some of their names, appearances, and aspects of their personal stories so they are not identifiable. Stories may include composite characters.

This paper meets the requirements of ANSI/NISO Z39.48-1992 (Permanence of Paper). This paper is SFI certified.

Library of Congress Control number: 2015940177
PR 17 16 15 14 13 12 11 10 9 8 7 6 5 4 3 2 1
ISBN 13: 9780795348488

For other life changing resources visit:
FloridaHospitalPublishing.com
FloridaHospital.com
CreationHealth.com

Contents

Introduction 8

Key One: Compelling Mission

1. Know Your "Why" 12
The Purpose of Mission

2. Think Long-Haul 28
Stewarding Your Mission

3. What The Best Companies Do 50
Balancing Your Mission

Section Summary: *Eleven Principles For Maximizing Your Mission Impact* 68

Key Two: Powerful Vision

4. Know Your "What" 72
Focusing Your Attention

5. Equipping Your Company for Greater Success 92
How Metrics Give Meaning to Vision

6. When It's Time for Your Vision to Change 112
What to Do so You Don't Settle for Average

Section Summary: *Twelve Tips On How Vision Drives Success* 132

Key Three: Critical Values

7. Behavior Must Match Words — 136
The Critical Place of Values

8. The Hazards Ahead — 156
How Values Serve as Guardrails to Protect from Serious Mishaps

9. Moving from the Head to the Heart — 176
How Good Values Help You Win Regardless of Uncertainty

Section Summary: *Ten Reasons Values Are Crucial* — 196

Key Four: Healthy Culture

10. Providing Favorable Conditions for Growth — 200
Lessons from a Petri Dish

11. Helping Your People Succeed — 220
Metrics Are Not Just about Better Numbers, but Personal Growth

12. Changing an Unhealthy Culture — 238
Don't Cut Off the Dog's Tail One Inch at a Time

Section Summary: *Ten Important Ideas Related to Your Company Culture* — 256

Key Five: Outstanding Leadership

13. Put On Your Armor 260
How to Survive and Even Thrive amid Criticism

14. Motivation Matters 280
Doing the Right Things for the Right Reasons

Section Summary: *Ten Insights about Outstanding Leadership* 296

Acknowledgments 298
About the Author 302
Notes 303

Introduction

FOR A LONG TIME NOW, I'VE WORKED IN SENIOR leadership roles in large organizations. I haven't managed a department or anything relatively small for well over two decades. The bulk of this book, therefore, is written from the perspective of someone who has spent a great deal of time in a senior leadership position; and yet, I want to discuss core issues that concern leaders of all sorts, from those who lead small groups all the way to those who lead large organizations. I believe the timeless principles discussed here apply to all leaders of all organizations, wherever they may serve on the leadership spectrum.

Second, although I've spent almost my entire career laboring within the context of tax-exempt organizations, the leadership principles we'll investigate apply to both for-profit and tax-exempt organizations. Key insights with universal application are unpacked following each section of the book. Third, my own perspective on leadership has grown primarily in the atmosphere of faith-based organizations, a fact that also flavors a great deal of what I have learned over the past three decades or more.

As I look ahead, I believe we are about to go through some testing times. The crucial lessons I have learned over the past twenty or thirty years—about reducing waste, good stewardship, living from the high moral ground that insists we have an obligation to operate as efficiently and innovatively as the most venerated for-profit company on the planet—will become as valuable to us as gold. And so I hope that my contribution to the ongoing leadership discussion may prove especially helpful to those who long to make a great difference for good in their own sphere of influence, wherever that is and regardless of the economic climate of the era.

The times may change, but the need for effective organizations committed to an outstanding mission never will. It is for them that I have written this book.

Don Jernigan

KEY ONE

COMPELLING MISSION

Here is the test to find out whether your mission on earth is finished. If you're alive, it isn't.

— Richard Bach

In This Section You Will:

- Learn how a succinct, strong, memorable, unchanging mission statement grounds an organization during changing times.

- Find out why a compelling mission statement can attract new recruits.

- Understand why relentless stewardship is as important for tax-exempt organizations as it is for for-profit companies.

- See how true success comes when money and mission intersect.

1

Know Your "Why"

The Purpose of Mission

BILL GEORGE, THE FORMER CHAIRMAN AND CEO of Medtronic, knows a thing or two about how to foster healthy business growth. In a dozen years under his leadership, Medtronic grew from a $1.1 billion company into a $460 billion behemoth—an average of 35 percent growth per year. George joined Medtronic in 1989 and in 2003 wrote a best-selling book, *Authentic Leadership,* based largely on his experience there.

"The best-kept secret in business," he wrote, "is that mission-driven companies create far more shareholder value than do financially driven firms. . . . It is only through a sense of purpose that companies can realize their potential."[1]

To illustrate his point, George contrasted the fates of two banks, Wells Fargo and U.S. Bancorp. For the decade prior to the publication of his book, Wells Fargo had focused on providing excellent customer service by expanding its network of banks in the Midwest and West. During the same period, U.S. Bancorp emphasized cost cutting and centralizing services, thus generating almost immediate profit increases and a rapid climb in stock. But because it had failed both to focus on its customers and on motivating its employees, the bank's profits soon plummeted and its stock lost more than half its value, prompting the company's sale to a smaller group. Meanwhile, Wells Fargo kept growing at a steady pace, even during a recession, and by the time George wrote his book, Wells Fargo had a value double that of U.S. Bancorp.

"Authentic leaders know that *only* by pursuing their missions with passion and commitment can they create sustainable value for their customers, their employees, and their shareholders," George concluded.[2] Medtronic's founder, Earl Bakken, back in 1962 had written a simple mission statement for his company: "To restore people to fuller lives." Five years before, despite creating the world's first pacemaker, the company teetered on the edge of bankruptcy. Bakken's board of directors urged him to write a mission statement, and that statement gave Medtronic a clear purpose and focus. Within just three months, the company became profitable, setting the stage for its remarkable growth under Bill George.

If your organization lacks a clear and compelling mission, then all I can say is, good luck. Because that mission, succinctly conveyed in a few memorable words, can spell the difference between success and failure, fulfillment and frustration.

My Journey to Purpose

Many years ago, I worked as a division manager for a publicly traded company. I enjoyed my work, liked and cared for my colleagues, and they seemed to feel the same way about me. But I stayed there only a couple of years.

I'd been hired essentially to lead a group of scientists who knew next to nothing about business management. While the company compensated me well and I enjoyed some real success, eventually I left for a cluster of reasons. But one single issue provided the overriding motivation for me to move on.

My corporate employer lacked any mission other than to make money for its shareholders. But I needed a strong motivation outside of finances to do my best work. Without such an element, I felt like I was dying inside. I had no passion for my work. Eventually the time came to move on; but I needed something more than a new job.

I needed a new *mission.*

What Is Mission?

Your mission supplies your purpose, your *raison d'être* (literally, "the reason for existence"). When you speak of your organization's "mission," you refer to its purpose for being, its designed intent. Your mission tells you what you're supposed to do, and so it usually explains why you became involved with your organization in the first place.

Vision, on the other hand, describes how you intend to fulfill your mission. Vision flows from mission, and the two must reinforce each other.

In addition, mission differs from vision in that a group's mission usually changes little, if at all, over time. A group's vision, by contrast, may look different from one period to the next, depending on prevailing circumstances and the style of the leader and his or her approach. Generally speaking, the mission of an organization will be either permanent or close to permanent, while its vision—its strategic plan for how to best fulfill that mission—may change significantly in response to shifting conditions, evolving ecosystems, or migrating audiences.

Fostering a strong sense of mission in your people will take your organization to a whole new level.

Organizations will have missions as different as their goals, hopes, and dreams.

Most for-profit companies, especially publicly traded ones, have relatively simple missions. Most of them focus on making a financial profit, both for the company and for the stockholders. Publicly traded companies raise capital by selling shares of stock. And who buys that stock? People who want to turn a profit. So when the company struggles, capital tends to move away in a hurry.

Compare that with tax-exempt organizations such as my own, Adventist Health System. Our mission statement is just seven words long: "To extend the healing ministry of Christ." We are primarily in the business of meeting the needs of our patients. That is why we exist. Our mission statement describes the reason why and how we take our particular approach to healthcare. Our mission motivates us and gives us a passion for caring for people and treating them as individuals, not as commodities. It motivates us to treat every patient—including the disheveled homeless man who walks into our emergency room in need of help—the way Jesus treated those he met, as valuable human beings created in God's own image.

> *Wasting a resource means you can no longer use it to do something good for your customers or constituency.*

Unlike for-profit corporations, we don't exist to make money or enrich our shareholders. We don't have shareholders. While many tax-exempt organizations have social missions, most faith-based groups, like our own, have what I call a *transcendent* mission. Adventist Health System, for example, is in the healthcare business to extend the work of the One we worship as divine, who came to bring healing and hope to a broken world. We carry on this work because we believe that the people who receive our care are God's children, designed to live forever.

Why Have a Mission Statement?

Why should every organization have an unchanging sense of mission and then work to develop a potent mission statement that clearly, succinctly, and compellingly describes that mission? You might as well ask, "Why should I have a clear idea of where I'm going?" If you don't care where you end up, then it doesn't particularly matter in which direction you go.

A clear sense of mission and a succinct, strong mission statement constantly puts into your mind a specific picture of why your organization exists, which in turn helps to keep you and the people who work with you focused on your organization's stated reason for being. Mission is an ideological compass to keep you moving in the righ t direction, a GPS unit designed to help you reach your desired destination.

Every initiative or enterprise that your organization launches should lift off from the platform of your own mission statement. That mission statement should strongly and concisely spell out why your organization exists (what you are in business to accomplish) in a way that inspires passion among everyone connected to your organization. The people in your organization need to know your mission statement, and that mission statement needs to *resonate* with them.

In our organization, I think you'd be hard-pressed to find an employee who can't tell you our mission statement. Someday, someone may come up with a more powerful, more emotionally engaging way to state our mission, but even if that should happen, the heart of our mission will remain the same. We exist, whether yesterday or today or tomorrow, to extend the healing ministry of Christ.

An unchanging mission, expressed in a memorable

mission statement, helps to ground an organization in a world that seems to change almost every twenty-four hours. In our specialized world of healthcare, people's basic human needs remain essentially the same, even though the way those needs get met can change profoundly and quickly. Ponder what's currently happening in the United States.

Over the past few years, this country has engaged in a great, crushing debate over healthcare reform. Some of the changes taking place will radically change how Americans receive healthcare. Not only that, but medical technology continues to advance with breathtaking speed, in the process creating some serious ethical questions, especially over end-of-life issues and who receives what kind of treatment and at what cost.

As important as mission is, never let a strong sense of mission excuse budget blindness.

No matter how society at large answers these tough questions, we will continue working to fulfill our unchanging mission. No doubt we will have to adjust *how* we fulfill that mission—that is, our vision and our expectations of that vision will change—but regardless of what comes down the pike, we will continue to labor to extend the healing ministry of Christ.

All organizations need a mission statement that serves a similar ageless purpose. In a world overrun with daily change, every organization needs their own North Star, an affirming purpose that gives meaning and direction.

Everybody needs motivation, and a great mission statement can provide an ample supply of it.

The Mission as Motivation

A nurse I'll call Renee worked in the emergency room at one of our hospitals. One evening, a man with diseased feet came into the ER, clearly requiring urgent attention. Renee fetched a wash basin, had the man sit down in front of her, and washed and treated his ailing feet. After she finished drying them, she told the man he would need some follow-up care.

"But I don't have any money to pay for it," he replied.

What happened next supplied an amazing example of our mission in action. Renee stood up, retrieved her purse, grabbed some cash, and gave it to the man, with no expectation of ever having it repaid. Talk about finding personal motivation in corporate mission!

Renee didn't act in this way because the emergency department director or a hospital administrator asked her to extend mercy to the poor man. Nor would anyone recommend that our staff act identically in every similar situation. Renee acted out of a heartfelt sense of compassion that she believed would emulate Christ in that particular case. In other words, she did what she did because she truly wanted to extend the healing ministry of Christ—our mission and hers. I am grateful for her, and for countless others like her, whose passion for our corporate mission motivates them to go the extra mile for our patients.

Add Vocation to Profession

Most of the people I work with consider themselves true professionals who find great personal satisfaction in their labors. But while I want our team to approach their work with an uncompromising attitude of professionalism, at the same time, I've learned that a *strictly* professional mindset can get in the way of a healthy mission mindset. When the professional mindset becomes an organization's ultimate focus, its people tend to stop right there. They don't move forward toward accomplishing the organization's stated mission. While they may do good work, they seldom do outstanding work.

How can you keep the men and women in your organization from falling into that kind of unfortunate rut? How can you motivate them to hold to high professional standards while at the same time remaining passionately committed to your mission?

I believe the professional mindset can work in beautiful union with the mission mindset, so long as the people in your organization complement it with a sense of calling. I call this phenomenon "adding vocation to profession," and I've seen it motivate people to approach their jobs with a profound sense of mission.

All companies, but especially tax-exempt organizations, can benefit in enormous ways by intentionally helping their people to add vocation to profession. I try hard to inculcate a sense of purpose in our own organization by doing everything I can to help people view our mission as a calling. I want to connect what we all do, regardless of the "size" or nature of our specific task, to something far bigger than the task itself.

Renee, the nurse in the story above, didn't care only for the immediate need of a hurting man's diseased feet; she sought to care for his future needs—at her own personal expense, with no expectation of return. She added vocation to profession by doing more than her employer would have required of her.

No matter what type of organization you provide leadership in, I encourage you to spend some time pondering whether your current mission statement does a good job of motivating your people to work for something much bigger than a mere paycheck. Do they see how their work contributes to something greater than themselves or greater than their boss's expectations? In my role as the CEO of a faith-based healthcare organization, I strongly believe in recognizing and celebrating my employees and the good work they do, but I believe even more strongly in fostering an attitude of purpose and meaning in work.

All men and women long to be a part of something much bigger than themselves.

Your organization may have a very different mission from ours, but let me challenge you as a leader to explore how to create a deeper sense of calling for your employees. Toward what sublime motivation or transcendent purpose can you point them? All men and women long to be a part of something much bigger than themselves, and most loathe

the idea of spending their careers with people who lack any greater vision than to promote themselves. How can you help them add vocation to profession?

This mix of profession and vocation also clearly affects the way my organization relates to other healthcare organizations. The existence of more than one major healthcare organization in a particular area often creates an atmosphere of unhealthy competition, but since we believe we have a divine calling and a unique mission, we know we have a distinctive reason for being. That frees us to be generous toward other healthcare entities that some might consider our competition. You might say that any enemy of our enemy (disease and ill health) is our friend. And we wish only the best for our friends. That's one of the things that adding vocation to profession can accomplish for an organization.

> *Money is nothing more than a means of measuring how you use your limited resources.*

A Great Recruiting Tool

Can a great mission serve as a recruiting tool for your company? I believe it can. For example, if you spent much time at one of our Adventist Health System hospitals, it would become apparent rather quickly that our mission attracts a high percentage of people of faith. Many of these people share our spiritual worldview, even though they represent a wide variety of faith congregations.

These professionals don't come to us because they're Adventists (most of them are not) or only because they need a job (often there are other choices). They join us because they like our mission and they admire the way we go about executing that mission. They believe that our *corporate* mission helps them fulfill their *personal* mission. And this combination makes them want to work with us as much as we want them to work with us.

I've been a patient at several of our hospitals, and I remember many late-night conversations with my attending nurses. On my last stay, I remember a nurse telling me, "I'm here practicing my profession because this organization supports my personal mission." She told me that throughout her nursing career, she's always loved to pray with her patients; she finds the practice gives many of her charges great comfort. But when her managers at a hospital in the Midwest found out about her offering to pray with patients, they threatened to fire her if she did not immediately take prayer out of her caregiving toolkit. She left before they could terminate her. Eventually she landed at one of our hospitals, where her practice of praying with willing patients was approved rather than censured.

"I just love being here," she beamed, "because I'm not only *allowed* to do that, I'm *encouraged* to do that if the patient wants it. This organization lets me live out my sense of mission."

Her statement reminded me of a simple truth: The fulfillment of any organizational mission starts within the heart and mind of each individual who works for that organization. It's one thing to put together a grand mission statement, to paste it all over the walls of your buildings, and to highlight it on your organization's web page. But it's something else altogether to find people who personally embrace the mission and who live out that mission in the real world.

No organization is better than the sum total of the individuals who work in it. And your organization's mission can come to life and grow only when the individuals who serve with you embrace it as their own vocation.

This has to happen on a personal level. An organization can't hand someone a sense of mission, as if it were some kind of assignment. But it can support and personalize a mission by creating an environment that encourages individuals to add vocation to their profession. As a leader, I encourage you to do whatever you can to help your people personalize their mission by providing them a central place of meaning that revolves around your corporate mission.

> *It is deadly to give any human being a free pass for spending someone else's money.*

I often hear my coworkers say, "All of us who work here are God's children, taking care of God's children." That is a meaningful statement, because it so personally links the caregiver and the patient. It also gives our employees far greater personal meaning in their work than simply seeing themselves as competent healthcare workers.

Nurses like the one who cared for me during my last hospital stay demonstrate how an organization can not only encourage employees to embrace the corporate mission, but at some point, help them make it their own.

Leaders Foster the Mission

Your organization won't develop a deep sense of mission on its own. You can't merely create a mission statement and then expect it to naturally permeate your organization. As a leader, you must make a concerted effort to make your group's mission *central* to who you are as an organization, and then find multiple ways to instill that mission within the individuals who make up your organization.

Successful leaders are active in making sure the mission of their organization permeates the culture of their organization. They accomplish this task primarily by focusing on three crucial activities:

- Constantly speaking about the mission everywhere within the organization
- Fostering an environment that embodies the mission
- Seeking out and training leaders who can attract and develop mission-focused employees—people who feel inspired by the mission and who therefore develop a passion to fulfill it.

I have found that nothing inspires people to embrace the mission of an organization like real-life stories, compelling tales that describe how men and women put specific actions behind the inspiring words. As a leader, you can help foster passion for your organization's mission by seeking out and telling (and retelling, and retelling) real-life tales of employees living out the mission.

In Adventist Health System, we go out of our way to communicate stories, starring both patients and caregivers, that inspire and motivate our people to personally embrace our mission. (You can read some of these stories on our Web page: www.AdventistHealthSystem.com/mission-stories).

A number of years ago I became CEO of one of the largest hospitals in our system. Not long after arriving I met with one of our executive vice presidents to talk about making changes that would further strengthen our focus on mission. I thought, for example, that our annual Golden Gala, a fund-raiser supporting important programs, needed to become more mission focused. I wanted to do all we could to make sure people came to the gala out of support for our mission, not because of the fantastic entertainment.

Balanced metrics support a strong mission.

I suggested we work to raise passion and support for our mission by telling stories featuring moving examples of how people in our organization have not just voiced support for our mission but have also lived it out. The strategy worked to a greater degree than any of us anticipated, and our fund-raising efforts have continued to grow. Does telling stories sound trivial? I assure you, it's not. Stories not only inspire people, they also help them to think about and embrace a sense of mission. People tend to better grasp truth when it comes attached to a story that deeply touches their hearts.

One thing to keep in mind, though, is that while true-life stories can inspire, encourage, and motivate the people who work in your organization, you can't rely exclusively on stories to tell the *whole* story of what's going on in your organization. Stories can describe only what happened at one particular time in one specific place. But even so, by recounting tales of people who went the extra mile to fulfill your organization's mission, you can inspire and motivate individuals to embrace your group's mission for themselves. Tears and laughter are great mnemonic devices.

Reach a Whole New Level

Of course, not everyone in your company will respond to the mission in the same way. Some may take to it quickly, while others may need more time to grasp it and buy into it. And still others may not embrace the mission at all (which may call for a parting of ways).

But no matter how difficult and time-consuming the work of instilling mission may be, keep at it. Fostering a strong sense of mission in your people will take your organization to a whole new level. Remember Bill George at Medtronic? He saw a strong mission take his for-profit company to a dozen years of 35 percent annual growth. What might doing something similar accomplish in your organization?

2

Think Long-Haul

Stewarding Your Mission

ALMOST IMMEDIATELY AFTER I FIRST WENT TO work in healthcare administration, I experienced something that shocked me. In my first year associated with a new organization and a new profession, the hospital I led booked a bottom-line loss of *$3 million*. . . and practically no one in the organization blinked.

By that time in my career, I had begun to acquire some decent business skills. When I started seeing all kinds of sloppiness and waste in the organization, I started asking questions. Often I got the same stinging reaction: "You're causing us problems, and you really don't understand our mission."

Now, I may have been a bad person, but I understood our mission very well; in fact, I strongly resonated with it. That's why I insisted we deal forcefully with our precarious fiscal situation. It took us two years and a lot of belt-tightening to pull out of our financial free fall, and by the end, most people had stopped calling me a bad person. But I still didn't quite know how to explain the changes and cuts I had overseen, other than saying, "If we don't do this, friends, we go out of business."

When I moved on from that job and took charge of several healthcare facilities in the same system, I saw a similar story played out there. Only a few of our institutions were generating surplus income; all the others had become financial parasites. Clearly, we could not sustain such an imbalanced system. All the money-losing facilities would eventually drag even the successful hospitals into bankruptcy.

When I brought these facts to the attention of the board, the members nodded at my sheets of paper and acknowledged the possibility of our financial peril, but they quickly moved on to discuss new projects, new equipment, and new facilities that would require large capital investments. They all assumed that the money would come from "somewhere." My colleagues didn't seem to realize that our financial problems threatened every service our system provided.

As I continued to talk internally about our challenges, everywhere I went I saw a persistent tendency to use our strong sense of mission to excuse our almost total budget blindness. After all, wasn't this a nonprofit institution? Wasn't this a system dedicated to serving people in the name of Christ? C'mon, Don, we're all about healing, not about making money.

But I'd seen the books, and I knew the money would dry up. I saw our entire system headed toward insolvency. We had to understand that if we wanted to stay afloat, we needed to start generating surpluses. In other words, if we were serious about our mission, then we had to get serious about our bottom line.

When I delivered that unsettling message, once more I got serious pushback. Most of my colleagues could give reasons for their substandard performance. And everywhere I described our shaky finances, I heard a familiar, unexamined assumption: People *really* committed to a charitable mission don't place much emphasis on fiscal performance. Since I didn't know what else to say, I repeated myself. "Listen," I said, "we are *not* going to use the system to ship money on a permanent basis from one community to another. *You* have to be accountable to generate *here* the resources you need to deliver a high-quality service to *this* community. Don't expect another institution to do your job for you."

> *Anyone who divorces mission from money should expect disaster.*

Truth be told, my own words made me feel more than a little schizophrenic. I didn't want to depend on a merely expedient argument: "Do this, or go belly-up." I had to figure out a way to describe the difficult task ahead that felt whole, healthy, and consistent. I simply couldn't function long term without believing that the mission I had so wholeheartedly endorsed did in fact guide my actions as a leader. I couldn't live with the tension in my soul of a split personality, where on the one hand I thought about all the good things taking place in our system—caring for patients, saving lives, bringing health to the community—and on the other hand I was the guy, hatchet in hand, who did whatever he thought necessary to secure the survival of his organization. And so I wondered, *Is there an organizing principle here?* I needed a new understanding of the problem facing us and a potent way to communicate that fresh idea to my coworkers.

I eventually found it in the counsel of Dr. William Cleverley, a professor at The Ohio State University specializing in healthcare finance. He's now president of Cleverley + Associates and continues to serve as an emeritus professor at OSU. He was a close mentor for several years, and in that time, he revolutionized how I looked at the world, at life, and at management. Through him, I learned the crucial principle of stewardship—a valuable concept for any leader, but especially for those who lead tax-exempt organizations.

Fuzzy about Finances

Before we dig into the principle of stewardship, perhaps we should ask why "not-for-profits" tend to struggle with this issue far more than do "for-profits." The simplest explanation is that a for-profit corporation has absolutely no ambiguity about its financial motivation.

In our society, people accept as a given that an investor-owned company exists to make money for its shareholders. Such an entity never forgets that it exists to create a profit. While it may make a wonderful product that provides some great social good, watch what happens when it suffers one or two bad quarters. Its great product and wonderful mission matters nothing if the organization fails to create value for its shareholders. For that reason, the CEOs of for-profit corporations walk on a high wire. They expect no mercy if they start consistently missing projections. No one has any ambiguity about that.

People within not-for-profit organizations, on the other hand, tend to get much more muddled about their group's finances. That's especially true if they work for an organization that operates on the basis of an altruistic, or even spiritual, mission statement. My own organization, for example, says that it exists to extend the healing ministry of Christ. What role should finances play in an organization like mine?

While it is a great and powerful privilege to lead in a nonprofit environment, in many ways, it's also much more difficult. Count on it: When you, as the leader of a nonprofit organization, start to talk about financial discipline, some of your people will reply, "Why are you even talking about that? This has nothing to do with our mission." That's hogwash, of course, but it's a reality that can create real problems within your organization.

The fact is that much of the looseness, sloppiness, and poor performance that plagues many not-for-profits develops because people within those organizations don't grasp the legitimate relationship between mission and money. That is, they don't understand the concept of stewardship. But you do yourself and your organization no moral good by divorcing mission and money. Both secular and faith-based not-for-profits need to be as strong and disciplined about this issue as any for-profit group in the world.

I continually tell our people that no for-profit should ever be more disciplined than we are. Since our mission is to extend the healing ministry of Christ, no one should have better business practices than we do. No one should do a better job in supply chain management than we do. We should be as efficient in our use of labor and resources as anyone on the planet. Why should our processes lag behind those whose primary motive is making a financial profit for shareholders? We cannot get muddled about the fact that we are fully accountable for what we do with the resources entrusted to us.

Some people will try to use the "high moral ground" of your mission to manipulate you into making "right" choices that in fact violate sound morality.

The Ancient Conflict

Early in my healthcare career, I observed an organizational dichotomy. Our clinical people—nurses, doctors, and other clinicians—tended to look askance at our financial people, and vice versa. The two groups tolerated one another but considered each other deficient in some significant way.

I've had great fun over the years attacking this diseased mindset. I have delighted in getting our clinical people and our financial people in the same room, and then revealing what they each think of the other. Without fail, by the end of our sessions, they're rolling in the aisles with laughter, more than a little embarrassed that their "secrets" have been so publicly exposed. And then I make them work together.

Although I'm no thespian, I thoroughly enjoy acting out each part. I'll say, "You clinical people say, 'We are the virtuous ones, the holy ones. We're the good people here. We're doing the Lord's work. We take care of sick people.' And then you look over at these financial types and you say, 'But we have this *other* group over here. They're really not very good people. They're money-grubbers, concerned only about the bottom line. They don't care about our patients, or about our mission, or about quality. They want us to make bricks without straw. They care only about finances—and some of that money is dirty.' "

A succinct, compelling mission statement can spell the difference between success and failure.

By this point in my little drama, the financial people usually have begun to snicker. But I don't let them gloat for long. I continue: "And here's what you financial people think about your clinical colleagues. You say, 'These folks might be good people, but they're airheads. They don't have a clue about money or what it costs to do anything. They don't care if we run out of funds or even if we go bankrupt. They have no clue about how to effectively manage money, and they couldn't care less if they waste resources. They're all a few bricks short of a load.' "

By now everybody's chuckling, and so I turn back to the clinical people and say, "I realize you folks consider yourselves the backbone of our organization. You're the angels, the ones who care. But I've noticed that you seem to enjoy cashing your paycheck, the same way that the accountants enjoy cashing theirs. And I haven't seen you volunteering to go without one. So if you really *are* all that holy, then why don't we just agree to donate our services to the community? Or at least take a 30 percent cut in pay? Holy people don't need nice paychecks, do they?"

By this time, we're all laughing. And then I know I can start educating them on the concept of stewardship.

"This is crazy," I insist. "I want financial people who care as much about the care of patients as the clinical people, and I want clinical people who have the skills and the knowledge to be good business people. *And I will not tolerate you thinking ill of each other.* We are one team with one mission, and the attitudes that you sometimes express toward each other are inherently un-Christian."

I let that statement sink in, and then I conclude, "There are no good people or bad people in this organization. There are only two kinds of people here—good stewards or poor stewards. It doesn't matter whether you work in a clinical area or a support area. You're either a good steward or a poor steward."

In my three decades of working in healthcare management, one of the things I'm proudest of is bringing together our clinical staff and our financial staff, getting them to work together in harmony. And once both groups begin to understand the crucial principle of stewardship, they really do start working together as a team.

Every Decision Is Sacred

The concept of stewardship revolutionized my thinking about how mission intersects with finances. It comes down to this: *Every decision is sacred.*

Money is nothing more than a means of measuring how you use resources. If you want to pursue your mission for only one year, then after carrying it out for 365 days, you can sell your organization and go out of business. But if you want to perpetuate that mission year after year, then you must find a way to deliver sufficiently high-quality outcomes that generate enough resources so you can pursue your mission indefinitely. And if anywhere in your organization you are wasting money, you are committing a crime against your mission—especially if you consider your mission to be a sacred one. For if your mission is sacred, so also are your resources needed to fulfill the mission.

> *People in both for-profit and tax-exempt organizations often fail to grasp the legitimate relationship between mission and money.*

Since a mission encompasses an entire ecosystem, we are stewards of every shekel that passes through our hands.

We are simply stewards of the resources that come to us.

I know of no concept more powerful on this issue than that of being a good steward. As a leader, every decision you make about how to use your resources is a sacred decision. You make either a good decision that allows you to do more good for more people, or you make a poor decision that wastes your resources and so prevents you from doing some good thing that you would like to have done.

So when someone says to you, "You care only about money; you don't care about our mission," the most powerful reply you can offer is to remind the individual about stewardship. It isn't about you. And it isn't about them. It's about how all of you, together, can more effectively use the limited resources you have to accomplish the mission you have accepted.

Stewardship must always be a part of the mission in any successful organization. Understood holistically, every action you take and every decision you make has ethical implications. This means that *everything* in your operation that affects your mission takes on sacred importance.

How Do You Get Them to Care?

Many organizations have employees or associates who have access to other people's dollars but little incentive to care about the group's bottom line. How do you get them to care?

We work with physicians in private practice who have a deep sense of stewardship; they work hard to avoid wasting resources. But we also work with others who have less of that sense. Imagine a surgeon who uses implantable devices. Suppose he feels no direct fiscal consequence for the decisions he makes regarding the devices he uses; the cost of the resource has no effect on him personally. Because he wants to keep his patients happy, he may want to use the most expensive implantable possible, even though the patient's welfare doesn't require it.

Let's get ridiculous for a moment. Suppose the physician decides to implant a platinum device that will remain in an uncorroded state for two thousand years—but the patient has a life expectancy of only fifteen years. That's how resources can get wasted. And that's the challenge.

Not long ago someone told me about an issue with some orthopedic providers. When he approached them to suggest their costs per case seemed high, they immediately responded, "Obviously, you don't understand orthopedics. We are giving the best patient care possible. And you don't care about good patient care. You care only about the bottom line."

I can't tell you how many times I've been burned by somebody spending my nickel. It is not good for the soul of human beings to have a free pass at spending somebody else's money. I consider it one of the curses of the community hospital model. I guarantee you, if you take that same physician and throw him into his own surgery center, he will immediately begin to behave differently. Potentially, he's spending his take-home pay, which he'll have to discuss every month with his spouse.

I believe you tread on dangerous ground anytime your system disconnects a human being from the financial consequences of his or her decisions. That's why we've worked so hard to develop models where we can incentivize (not penalize) physicians to make the best decisions. We want them to make the optimal decision, fully considering the needs of the patient and the desire to do the most good for the most people over the longest period of time. So if at all possible, give every employee or associate some accountability for the net results of your tax-exempt organization's work.

If you are a leader in a 501(c)(3), think of your organization as "tax exempt" rather than as "not-for-profit."

Moral High Ground

As leaders, we must think deeply about our moral compass, our moral reasoning, about what's right and wrong in the context of our unique systems. We can't afford to be superficial here. I tell my managers, "Using good management principles that generate the resources you need to spend capital in this community is exactly the right thing to do. It is morally wrong to expect another organization (or department, or associate) to subsidize your poor management."

We can avoid some of the confusion about the high moral ground when we move from the thirty thousand–foot level down to the ten-foot level. In our case, we talk about what specific things nurses, doctors, and support staff on individual units can do to improve care while lowering costs. I don't ask them to compromise the care they give; quite the contrary. I say, "We're going to deliver superior care that's also more efficient. In so doing, we will lower the burden of healthcare costs so that our community can afford decent schools, roads without potholes, functioning sewers, and well-staffed police departments."

To waste a resource means that we can no longer use it to do something good for our community. Since we get to spend our resources only once, living with a stewardship mentality has profoundly moral implications. And living wastefully is profoundly immoral.

When I worked at my first hospital, I could have visited a good friend at one of our profitable organizations and said to him, "Would you please ship money to us for the next twenty years and subsidize our operation?" He loves me, but I know what he would have said. "No," I can hear him retort, "I'm not willing to do that." In fact, it would have been *immoral* for him to do that. Nobody gave him permission to take limited healthcare resources from one community and ship them to another community, particularly when we already had several good hospitals in our area. My friend occupied the high moral ground, even though he didn't have to use it.

Others, however, *will* try to use the high moral ground of your mission to manipulate you into making choices that seem "right" but in fact violate sound morality. Not long ago, I received an invitation to speak at a joint meeting of clinical and financial executives. I'd been informed that some members of these groups had started to play the game, "What Is the Most Moral Position?" in order to squash further discussion. I began my presentation like this:

> I want to describe two conditions to you. Please listen very carefully. Here is State A: our health system is in the top decile in the united states on any named metric of quality and safety, and our cost to provide healthcare is x. Here is State B: our health system is in the top decile in the united states on any named metric of quality and safety, and our cost is x minus 20 percent. Which of the two states is the most moral state?

I didn't ask my audience to name the most "effective" state or the "best business position" or "the best state for the financial future of our health system." I asked them to identify the most *moral* state. And they all "got it." They answered correctly, "State B."

I congratulated them and then insisted, "You cannot divorce finance from your clinical product, because finance is simply a way of measuring the resources you use to produce a given state. Therefore, if you try to divorce the questions of finance and quality, then Number One, you're being extremely unwise; and Number Two, your organization is in for some really ugly outcomes in the not-too-distant future."

While I believe with all my heart in the quality agenda, I abhor loose, lazy, sloppy thinking that divorces the question of creating a high-quality product from doing the hard work of delivering that product at ever lower costs. Both sides of the equation are equally "moral." Wastefulness robs a needy person of some beneficial outcome. And isn't that immoral?

Years ago when I managed a single hospital, I spoke at all the new employee orientation sessions so that I could discuss our mission. I would ask, "What good would it do to say to someone, 'I love you and God loves you' if our outdated CT scan causes us to miss a lesion on someone's mother, who then dies of treatable cancer? Would it make it any better that you had said, 'God loves you and we love you'? No. That would only make a mockery of your faith. And that's why I insist we discuss our use of resources. We want the best technology. We want nice facilities. We want to carry out our mission over many years. We want to be financially stable. And since that's all a part of the equation, we have to constantly look into improving our processes and making them more efficient so that we don't waste our limited resources."

Telling real-life stories that clearly illustrate your mission can help your organization to reach a whole new level.

In the business of healthcare, the stakes are enormously high. That's why I believe nobody should have better processes than we do. We need the most effective, efficient, and highest quality systems we can produce, at the lowest cost we can manage. It's a moral question. If we fail, then society at large will suffer. If we fail, we will see ugly rationing and many thousands of more people without access to healthcare—all because we were either too lazy or too stupid to create it.

I don't know of a higher moral platform than that.

The Intersection of Doing Good and Doing Well

In my view, the most successful organizations constantly look for the intersection of doing good and doing well. If you keep your mission in mind even as you continually look for ways to generate surpluses, then your resources will extend further. You'll be able to do more good than organizations that don't operate in this way. You will enjoy financial stability so that you don't lurch from crisis to crisis, so you can attract the best people. And when you attract the best people, you can plan an exciting future together.

I've been on the other side of that scenario, and I've seen the pain it causes. I have witnessed the terrible human toll on people and on communities when mission-driven organizations lack good stewardship. But I've also seen the wonderful things that can happen when organizations chartered for the public good take stewardship seriously.

Several years ago, when I was president of a large hospital, we decided to set up a clinic to care for patients without health insurance who suffered from congestive heart failure. The average incidence of hospitalization for this group in a given two-year period was astronomical. They had no quality of life to speak of; they seemed to just hang on. They frequently got readmitted because they lacked the resources to follow the regimens that offered them the best chance of getting healthier. After studying the problem, we set up the outpatient clinic.

After the clinic had operated for some time, I reported to the board on its amazing success. If you were there and weren't crying, you had no heart. These patients suddenly had hope. They saw they could have a decent existence, that they could do things they never dreamed of doing . . . and all because they received good aftercare.

That clinic is a case of doing good. But it also represents a case of doing well. We were spending *far* less money on treating these patients because we had dramatically reduced their incidence of hospitalization. Every time they wound up in our hospital, they needed all the expensive resources that accompany a four-to-six-day stay. We increased our profitability by reducing a major loss.

The most successful organizations constantly look for the intersection of doing good and doing well.

Through the clinic, we were able to significantly improve the lives of patients already in our care by using medical interventions we knew how to employ. We did "good" for our patients and we did "well" by our organization—a terrific example of stewarding our mission.

"Tax Exempt," Not "Nonprofit"

Throughout this chapter, I've used the term "not-for-profit" to describe organizations like ours, but the more accurate phrase is "tax exempt." We are chartered by the state to benefit society in some specific manner, and so we are exempt from certain taxes that other corporations must pay.

We unwisely tend to throw around the terms "nonprofit" or "not-for-profit" in such a way that some individuals in our organizations think that even to discuss money is somehow antithetical to the values of the organization. Unfortunately, such a wrongheaded attitude often leaks to the outside world.

Over the past several weeks, the major newspaper in our city has published a string of articles that imply the term *nonprofit* describes organizations that operate on a shoestring. The stories suggest that the typical nonprofit barely survives and, in fact, should not consider any financial issues in its organizational equation. I find it most regrettable that we have allowed such a misconception to exist. We've even created much of it.

We never should have used the term *nonprofit* to describe ourselves, but rather employed the more accurate term, "tax exempt." I recently told our executives, "I don't want to hear the word *not-for-profit* come out of your mouths ever again. You need to start referring to us and envisioning us as a tax-exempt organization."

One of the biggest financial supporters of the largest hospital in our system is a very wealthy man. He recently declared, "The term *not-for-profit* is not a business philosophy; it's a tax status." He understands that a well-run 501(c)(3) can do a lot more good in a community than can an organization struggling to survive. He supports us because he sees a successful business operation, with resources generated by our operations reinvested in the organization and in the community.

The real question for us must be: "Do we operate in such a way that we deserve a tax exemption? Do we deserve our tax exemption by what we do, how we do it, and whom we serve?"

Since this is one of the rare instances in which I believe a distinction in terminology is important, I will plan for the rest of this book to use the term *tax exempt* instead of *nonprofit* or *not-for-profit* when referring to such organizations.

The Need for Vigilance

Some time ago, a couple of executives in our organization came to me independently and asked, "How do you deal with people who say, 'We *have* to do this and we won't debate it, because anything else would be immoral and would betray our mission. If you question this, then we'd almost have to say you are not a Christian.' "

Both times, I burst out laughing.

With hurt and confusion in their eyes, they demanded, "Why are you laughing?"

"Welcome to leadership," I replied (still trying to stifle a chuckle). What I meant was, "Welcome to leadership in a faith-based organization."

It's amazing how often "religious" people will question your leadership motives when you ask questions about money, efficiency, and appropriate financial decisions. They say, "That doesn't seem consistent with our mission. You shouldn't even be raising those kinds of questions." But I always insist that *those very questions* are critically important to our mission, because we are stewards of all the resources placed in our hands, so we are going to ask *all* the questions that need to be asked. The moment I let someone shut down an important discussion, we have begun rumbling down the road to Big Time Trouble.

Strive to make your organization's mission central to who you are and what you do.

I simply won't abide behavior that attacks the motivation of those willing to ask hard questions, because such attempts to silence debate are deeply unhealthy. They imply that the would-be silencer knows something dark and unsavory about the commitment of the questioner—and I never let anyone get away with that poisonous game. Leaders need to remain vigilant here, because the issue keeps resurfacing.

A couple of years ago, I became convinced that the old imbalance had started to creep back in. As we increasingly focused on quality and safety, people naturally started to tilt in that direction.

We had a consultant who we hired to help us improve our quality and safety in one of our hospitals. But I learned he'd start meetings by saying, "How long are you going to keep killing people? Don't you care that you're killing them?" I told the CEO of that hospital, "That man would do that one time with me, and only one time." If I thought the motivation of our people had gone awry, if somehow we no longer cared about doing our sacred duty and caring for people in the best way we knew how, then I might have let such a comment pass. But since I knew that was far from the truth, I considered the statement incredibly damaging.

That consultant was using our mission against us. And if you as a leader allow that kind of thinking to take root, then before long, you'll descend to the same kinds of pathological behaviors that took our entire health system close to bankruptcy in the early 80s.

Extend Your Mission

Our responsibility is to use wisely whatever resources come within our sphere of influence, eliminating waste everywhere we can. If we do that, then we can do more good for more people in the long run. We will build up a balance sheet strong enough to invest for down times. And when we need to borrow money, our strong balance sheet will enable us to do so at low interest rates.

The financial strength that comes through good stewardship allows you to extend your mission to the maximum degree possible. Bad business decisions that end up wasting the organization's money, or allowing sloppy processes and inefficient procedures to continue, corrupt your own soul and hinder your organization's ability to fulfill its mission.

Constantly strive to teach the principle of stewardship to your employees. Teach them to understand that what they're doing, regardless of their organizational level, has consequences for your entire effort. Help them to see their personal impact on the recipients of your services, on the resources that they use, and on the influence that they wield. Help them to grasp the great significance of their work. Remind them of the effect they have on your organization's ability to remain stable financially and so fulfill its mission for years to come.

3

What the Best Companies Do

Balancing Your Mission

VICES HIDE IN THE SHADOWS OF OUR VIRTUES. It's a scary and profound thought, isn't it? I wish I'd come up with it, but I confess I didn't. I first encountered it years ago when I read a long-out-of-print book titled *The Seven Deadly Virtues.* Author Gerald Mann looked at seven classic virtues and showed how each one, taken to an extreme, gets twisted into an ugly and hurtful version of itself. Even your best strengths, in other words, can become your worst weaknesses if you fail to find a healthy balance.

Great virtues can have dark sides, indeed.

In a staff talk a few months ago, I used a story from Mann's book to illustrate the need for balance. Mann wrote of "God's Gestapo," of well-meaning people who take the good desire to act in an upright way and distort it into something noxious by divorcing the virtue of morality from the virtue of love.

Mann contrasted their skewed approach with the one his grandmother chose. She wanted her grandson to act in an upright way, but she didn't harangue him about bad behavior. Rather, she consistently appealed to his "better angel." One day, a teenaged Mann planned with his buddies to take advantage of his parents' absence by sneaking out of his grandma's house to get drunk, among other things. The boys had everything all planned . . . and then Grandma walked into his room, sat down on the bed next to him, and spoke of how blessed she felt to have such a wonderful grandson. She went on and on about how he always treated her so kindly and with such respect. She finished by declaring how deeply grateful she felt to count him as her grandson, an amazing young man she knew she could trust.

And just like that, Mann's night was ruined. He came home early that evening, as sober as a judge.

But what might have happened, Mann wondered, had his grandmother laid on the guilt and the shame and the finger-wagging? What if she had allowed the virtue of moral behavior to obliterate the virtue of grace? His life might have turned out very differently than it did (he grew up to become a pastor).

Unbalanced virtues can become unhinged vices—and this can happen both in our lives and in our institutions. Even organizations with outstanding mission statements can go bad. When they allow their mission to get out of balance, they risk falling into decline. Imagine a huge and beautiful archway held up on one side by a massive stone pillar . . . and on the other side by a few scrawny toothpicks hastily taped together. Would you want to stand next to such a structure?

I've learned through hard experience that *every* good impulse must be watched carefully. I remember all too well the many anxious mornings I've awakened with just one thought clawing at my brain: *How did we get to this awful place? How could we be facing this kind of crisis?* This isn't mere theory for me. I've seen it, breathed it, and lived it.

"But Don," someone asks, "can an *excellent* mission really kill an organization?" Yes, it can, if you allow it to get out of balance. I frankly love the mission of Adventist Health System. I can hardly imagine a more exalted mission than *to extend the healing ministry of Christ.* Who could have a loftier healthcare mission than that? And yet, in times past, we almost went out of business because we allowed that very mission to get out of balance.

Beware of Silos

I've seen terrific healthcare organizations that focused so strongly around a single dimension of success that they could no longer fulfill their mission. While they could proudly point to one remarkable area of strength, their mediocre (or even poor) performance in every other area made it difficult for them to survive. A good leader needs to focus on the whole picture.

A few years ago, a respected healthcare organization with a deserved reputation for outstanding patient experience approached us to see whether we might consider a merger. The

CEO of the institution had become famous by writing about his group's outstanding work in that specific dimension of healthcare. Its leaders told us they knew they lacked the funds to reach a new future, and they wondered if we might help them cross that bridge. We happily sent a team to investigate the possibilities, but it didn't take long for us to say, "Thanks for the offer, but no."

We discovered that while this organization had glowing numbers on patient experience, it had neglected nearly everything else. Outside of that one area, it had almost nothing to offer. When we looked at safety metrics, quality outcome metrics, strategic positioning, market share advantage—at just about anything but patient experience—the organization came up woefully short. Its great position on that single cherished metric didn't translate into other advantages. Its hardcore outcome numbers on crucial metrics like mortality, infections, and complications looked average at best. It appeared to us as though the institution would almost certainly go under without an immediate influx of significant cash. And we wanted no part of that.

> *A strong sense of mission keeps you focused on your organization's reason for being and headed in the right direction.*

That's what imbalance will do to you, regardless of the loftiness of your mission. Ignoring the essential elements of your mission will always result in serious consequences.

Every organization, even those with an exalted mission, must work to keep a balanced scorecard.

Balanced Metrics Support a Strong Mission

Every organization must have balanced metrics that define the group's success. Institutions get into trouble when their metrics grow unbalanced—which often happens when zealous people use the group's mission to nudge the organization toward imbalance. These zealots don't mean to do harm, but they will literally take your mission and twist it, thus destroying the balance your organization needs to thrive.

Our Florida Division hospitals have established "five pillars" to try to prevent such a disastrous imbalance. Our executives continually look at each of those five pillars to ensure that their mission stays in balance. The pillars include the crucial areas of finance, quality and safety, service, market, and team. We monitor *all* of these pillars *all* the time.

> *The work of balancing your mission never ends.*

I sometimes speak to our people about "the zone of stability." If our balance sheet doesn't stay within that zone, the resulting imbalance will, at some point, negatively impact patients. If we were to ignore operating costs in favor of an unbridled quest for quality and safety, for example, we would have to ignore waste and inefficiency. And then what would happen? Our operating margins would fall. Assuming we would be unwilling to totally lose our credit ratings, we would then have to slow our capital spending. We would need to delay the replacement of outdated CTs and MRIs and aging hospital wings. We would have to postpone acquiring new technology and put off starting that fabulous new service. And all of that, of course, affects patients very seriously. A balanced ecosystem requires a balanced approach to mission.

When I returned to Orlando in the early 90s to head up our system's multistate division, I came with a conviction that we had not spent enough corporate energy in the critical areas of quality and safety. Today, I feel proud of the strides we've made since then. I believe we desperately needed to focus on those areas.

But I have a confession to make. I wanted to do this, in part, because I firmly believed the time would come when the only way for us to significantly reduce our costs would be to improve our quality and safety metrics. I knew that if we did not improve those things, our failure eventually would cost us a lot of money.

I've always believed that a close connection exists between quality and financial efficiency. Poor quality is always inherently more expensive, while excellent quality typically delivers the best financial return. Ponder the last couple of decades in the automobile industry. Why did US automakers get clobbered? The simple answer is that Japanese and German firms figured out how to make a superior product. They significantly reduced waste and designed a manufacturing process in which variance got engineered out. And when variance gets engineered out, you wind up with a reliable car. The best organizations never apologize for going after both efficiency and quality, all of the time.

Seeking Philosophical Balance

Faith-based organizations almost always have a strong commitment to some particular theological perspective or philosophical outlook. Their members want to work with like-minded people. But the leaders of such groups need to remember that if we wish to fulfill our mission, we often need the help of people of good character who can enthusiastically endorse our mission, even if they cannot walk in lockstep with us on every philosophical point.

I think of one hospital that wanted to keep its underlying philosophy of mission "pure" by hiring only men and women who agreed *at every point* with that philosophy. A group of influential physicians at the core of this organization shared a very narrow perspective. A much larger group of excellent physicians who worked with them said, "Although we agree with you on 80 percent of your beliefs, you haven't been willing to recognize us as full-fledged members. But if you will simply let us join you, we will help you to make

> *When mission properly intersects money, every decision becomes sacred.*

this into a great institution. We can be loyal to your core mission, and we will not in any way interfere with what you want to do beyond it." The core group replied firmly, "No."

This group of "outsider" physicians, all of them high-quality professionals, represented perhaps 80 percent of that hospital's market. They reluctantly left and established a competing hospital a few miles away. The huge vacuum created by their departure instantly left the "philosophically pure" institution with a horrible financial problem; it simply didn't have enough business volume to sustain itself. In order to fix the financial hole, the hospital asked another set of physicians—a group far less accomplished professionally and much further away philosophically than the ones who left—to come in.

That hospital soon began to gain a reputation for mediocre care. The larger community noticed, of course, and voted for the new institution with its feet and checkbooks. While a few high-quality physicians remained at the original hospital, their numbers couldn't begin to compare with the large group of excellent physicians now staffing the new hospital. In a short period of time, the original hospital imploded. It simply couldn't compete.

Ironically, the old hospital stood in a part of the city that soon mushroomed in population. That hospital could have become a dominant provider of care in a growing, important city. It could have continued to fulfill its outstanding mission and even found ways to extend it. But because a core group of leaders lacked balance in regard to the organization's fine mission, it lost everything. Today, it's history. Kaput! And in any language, that's a shame.

Develop a Balanced Leadership Team

Like everyone else, leaders have both strengths and weaknesses. Many best-selling business books counsel leaders to focus on their strengths, since it takes an extraordinary amount of effort to improve even marginally in one's areas of weakness. Tom Rath's *StrengthsFinder 2.0* and Marcus Buckingham's *Now, Discover Your Strengths* represent this line of counsel.

While I have no quarrel with either the research or the conclusions in such books, I do insist that personal strengths, taken to an extreme, can become a significant problem. Someone asked me recently, "How can I as a leader keep from focusing my organization [or department or area of responsibility] on my one or two areas of greatest strength? How can I keep from falling into bad habits in the other areas, in which I have real weakness?"

I'm afraid I may have answered a little too bluntly. "All I can say," I replied, "is that's a lousy board and a lousy leader. Period. End of story. It should never happen." I meant that every CEO needs a strong board that insists on a balanced leadership team. That team, in turn, needs to operate according to some balanced measures of success.

Frankly, in some ways, your particular strengths or weaknesses are immaterial; it's really a question of the strength of your whole team. Any leader who stocks a leadership team with people just like him or her is headed for trouble. It's inevitable. Leaders have to be disciplined enough to say, "I know this isn't my strong suit, so I'm going to make sure I have individuals on my team who can do well the things that I can't. I'm going to put together a balanced team, even if my personality doesn't necessarily jibe with every member of my team."

As I think back over my career, I see that at nearly every major stop along the way, I put together internally cohesive and mutually supportive teams. I got incredible enjoyment out of working alongside most of the individuals who directly reported to me (I'd judge better than 80 percent of them). But almost always, I've placed someone on my team who I didn't particularly enjoy managing. I didn't look forward to one-on-one meetings with these individuals in the same way I did with everyone else, mostly because of personality differences. Still, I believed passionately that they needed to be a part of my team, I had the highest respect and regard for them, and I knew I absolutely needed them.

A compelling mission statement can serve as a great recruiting tool.

If you don't have this kind of dynamic on your leadership team, at least to some degree, then you ought to worry. It suggests to me that you want around you only those individuals whose personality styles "click" with your own, men and women with whom you can be best buds. And I seriously doubt that's healthy.

Gather a *balanced* team around you, and empower each member to make ethical, good choices. Embolden them to make hard decisions, and don't try to pretend or bluff your way through areas outside your area of expertise. Instead, learn to rely on whoever you put in key positions.

Make sure they know you'll hold them accountable for their decisions. As the key people to whom you've given great responsibility, tell them, "This is your job. This is why you're in a position of leadership. Yes, I understand you have to make some tough decisions, but this is your area of expertise. This is why you're here."

Finally, make it clear that you will give them your unqualified support. Make sure they know you will support them in their decision-making process. Don't let them worry that you'll hang them out to dry if something unexpected goes awry. If they've done their homework, followed your directives, and followed the course suggested by their expertise, then you'll back them 100 percent.

In the healthcare industry, a typical CEO is a good business leader who knows how to inspire the organization's employees around a compelling mission and vision. He or she probably doesn't have a clinical background, since such leaders rarely come up through that discipline. One of the most critical of all leadership positions in the healthcare industry, however, is the person who oversees patient care. Hospitals and clinics "do mission" essentially through the care of their patients—and that means the CEO had better have a *very* strong chief clinical officer, and then give him or her unqualified support.

Whenever I took over as CEO of a hospital, I typically interviewed the organization's key physicians. I wanted to hear from the ones known internally as the real movers and shakers, those whom everyone respected, the core players who seemed the most invested in the organization. One time when I scheduled such an interview, I had an encounter with a physician known not only for his clinical expertise, his outstanding care of patients, and his extraordinary talent as a clinician, but also for his strong opinions. He immediately began spewing a litany of chronic problems with the medical staff. He clearly thought that the organization had long protected certain staff members who had not performed up to acceptable standards. "What are you going to do about it?" he demanded.

Any system that disconnects human beings from the financial consequences of their decisions invites disaster.

I responded with a fervor that matched his intensity: "I am not a physician. I am not capable of fairly judging clinical outcomes; I expect the medical staff to do that. I expect them to do their job." I then added, "If you will do it, and you will do it right and you will do it fairly, then I will guarantee you—*guarantee* you—unequivocal backing for everything you decide. I don't worry the least about someone suing me. My job is to back you to the hilt; it's your job to make the correct and fair judgment." Over the next few years, all of his concerns got cleaned up.

It's funny what happens when the message finally gets around that sloppiness and poor performance will no longer be tolerated. You start to witness a sea change in the culture of the organization. All the clinical leaders begin to see that a new day has arrived, that management intends to hold everyone's feet to the fire—*everyone's*—and that it will accept nothing less than competent professionals doing their best to get it right.

The Need for Funnels

How does a leader funnel this emphasis on balance to the front line, to the workers who have direct contact with customers or clients?

Begin by recognizing that your sphere of leadership influence goes only so far. Don't kid yourself. *Your most critical task is to influence those who report directly to you.* Influence your direct reports and get them on board. Bring them to the place where they're with you not just because they want to keep their job, or because they fear you, but because they believe in balance as much as you do. In that way, they'll become as motivated, as fired up, and as committed to it as you are. That's your job number one.

I've been fortunate in that I've inherited situations in which, 90 percent of the time, I could pretty quickly get my direct reports on board. I didn't often have to make significant changes to get there. And once I did get there, I could stand back and witness something like a nuclear chain reaction. My people got their people on board, and the health I needed to see in my organization started sweeping through the whole place.

What can you do, however, if your direct reports do not quickly get on board, and you don't have the luxury of immediately cleaning house? In that case, you may have to work around your managers (but do so only as a short-term, emergency strategy).

From personal experience, I can tell you it's vastly easier to do this in an organization with a few hundred employees than one with thousands. If you have, say, twenty middle managers along a typical bell-shaped curve, then for a period of time, you can bypass them. In emergency situations, I did exactly that through town hall meetings in which I repeatedly met directly with employees. I did so because I found myself in a situation in which the managerial structure had become highly dysfunctional, and yet I didn't want to fire all my managers, because all of them didn't need firing. Still, we had to change a lot of bad habits. Through our town meetings, I gradually got the rank on file on board, and then the managers who "got it" worked to replace their bad habits with good ones. And at that point I could deal decisively

> *Financial discipline and a strong mission work together to help an organization thrive.*

with the managers who simply couldn't or wouldn't change.

Town hall meetings take a lot of time, however, and I've used them only as a last resort. It's far better and vastly more efficient to get your direct reports on the same page with you than to bypass them in an effort to change company-wide habits. If you need to hold town hall meetings in order to save the patient, then by all means, hold them. But do so only when necessary, and only for the shortest amount of time required. Make it your top priority, always, to get your direct reports moving with you, because that's where you'll achieve your greatest success.

It Takes Work to Find Balance

Balancing your mission takes never-ending work. You never reach a point where you can say, "Whew. Glad that's done. Now I don't have to worry about *that* anymore." We naturally tend to swing from one pole to the other; and to make things even more interesting for tax-exempt organizations driven by a strong mission, some common but unexamined assumptions often end up hurting us.

Church-related institutions, for example, frequently behave as though it's inherently unholy to make employees (and especially volunteers) face difficult realities. They see it as somehow inappropriate to demand performance, to require accountability, to expect excellence.

And tax-exempt institutions of all stripes, whether secular or religious, typically place compassion and caring at the core of their values. That's their *modus operandi.* They focus on a certain areas of service, whether that service involves the environment, political prisoners, exploited women, disabled veterans, impoverished third-world families, or whatever the target group might be. Leaders of these organizations typically bring a tolerant, supportive mindset to their task. It's all about philanthropy, after all. But then the notion creeps in that if you're *truly* charitable, you accept whatever level of performance you get. *Certainly,* you don't judge.

Frankly, I don't see how such a notion helps a service organization succeed in the long run. And I think it confuses "being nice" for "being gracious." The two are not the same. In fact, consider the example of someone who, through history, has developed a reputation for world-class compassion: Jesus Christ. No matter what you think about him, the record of his life shows that Jesus seemed to truly care about those in need. Many people, believers and nonbelievers alike, have examined his life and the way he interacted with his closest associates. In those interactions they have seen something more than tolerance. While he was unfailingly gracious, he was not always warm and fuzzy.

All through the gospels, you see Jesus reaching out to needy people with acts of grace and compassion. But you also see him challenging his colleagues to step higher, to better reflect Kingdom priorities, to become more effective in God's service.

He had to help his twelve core partners move past their own significant weaknesses. He had a chronic doubter named

Thomas. He had two hot-tempered brothers named Andrew and John. He had a follower named Matthew trained in the corrupt Roman world of collecting unjust taxes. And he had one fellow who could never seem to get his foot out of his mouth, named Peter. *These* were the leaders who would have to carry on Jesus's mission after his death.

So day after day, mile after mile, through dusty village after dusty village, Jesus trained these men how to move their performance past their limitations and inadequacies. "Take the next step. Move higher. Overcome." While he never stopped loving his associates, the ways he worked with them and the things he said to them didn't always seem "nice." While he could be very tender, he also knew how to confront. He did whatever seemed necessary to get through to someone. Sometimes that meant getting very blunt and even harsh in order to penetrate the thick artifice that we humans tend to build around ourselves. "Get behind me, Satan," doesn't sound very "nice," but he once said it to a dear friend when that's what it took to move the man to the next level.

Your mission is an ideological GPS unit.

As a leader, it's your duty and your calling to demand excellence—for the right reason, for the right purpose, and with an attitude that says, "We're going to demand the best that human beings can produce, but we're going to care for each other while we're doing it."

It's your job as a leader to keep your organization balanced. Occasionally that's no fun. Sometimes it's not popular. And frequently, people will misunderstand.

But that's the job.

I like what Paul Boese once said: "We come into this world head first and go out feet first; in between, it is all a matter of balance." To succeed as a leader, you must bring balance to your organization. If you don't want to go out feet first before your time (in terms of your leadership of a particular group), you'll make achieving this balance a top priority.

Section Summary

Eleven Principles For Maximizing Your Mission Impact

1. A strong sense of mission keeps you focused on your organization's reason for being and keeps it headed in the right direction.

2. A potent mission statement has an unmatched ability to motivate members of your organization.

3. A compelling mission statement can serve as a great recruiting tool.

4. Telling real-life stories that clearly illustrate your mission can help your organization reach a whole new level.

5. Anyone who divorces mission from money should expect disaster. Money is nothing more than a means of measuring how you use your limited resources.

6. Constantly look for the intersection of doing good and doing well.

7. In *both* for-profit companies and tax-exempt organizations, relentless stewardship expects performance, accountability, and excellence of employees (and volunteers).

8. Focusing too strongly on a single dimension of success can jeopardize your mission.

9. The best ally you have in bringing needed change to your organization is your unbending commitment to the organization's mission.

10. If you use wisely whatever resources come within your sphere of influence, eliminating waste wherever you can, you will do more good for more people in the long run.

11. When mission properly intersects money, every decision becomes sacred.

KEY TWO

POWERFUL VISION

Vision is the art of seeing things invisible.

— Jonathan Swift

In This Section You Will:

- Realize how a daring vision can powerfully motivate your *entire* organization to strive together toward a common goal.
- Discover three reasons why every great vision must partner with appropriate robust metrics.
- Understand why the tension most organizations experience when good metrics are applied to their group's processes and outcomes is healthy.
- Learn three symptoms that your organization's vision needs to change, and five steps to accomplishing such a change.
- See that innovation has a crucial role in relentless stewardship, which enables your organization to better fulfill its mission.

4

Know Your "What"

Focusing Your Attention

When I first arrived as the new leader of one large hospital, it didn't take long for me to realize that we faced a legion of serious challenges. We had more problems than I could easily keep track of, and I heard about them almost daily.

Physician after physician marched into my office to voice displeasure over the state of the hospital. Nearly all of them used words such as "unhappy," "uncomfortable," and "miserable" to describe their feelings. "Something has to change," several of them told me. "This isn't working. I need something different."

Within about three years, we had addressed most of those problems. The litany of common complaints had largely dried up; we had come a long way. At a leadership retreat, I looked around and marveled at just how far we had come. I pondered some of the big challenges we still faced moving forward, but I also contemplated the countless blessings we already had enjoyed. We were operating in a fantastic market, had an incredible share of that market, and had earned an off-the-charts reputation as a trusted healthcare provider, with well-known, high-quality programs and several world-class physicians.

And then it struck me, almost out of the blue. We needed a fresh, potent vision that would motivate us to charge boldly into the future. And so I made an impromptu announcement.

"The vision of this organization," I declared, "should be to become a global pacesetter delivering preeminent, faith-based healthcare." As I scanned the audience, I wondered how people would react. Nobody laughed. Nobody groaned. Nobody shrieked. But I saw a lot of smiles and confident, nodding heads. I think at that moment we all felt ready for an exciting new challenge, and such an audacious vision statement seemed to fit the bill.

The Need for Vision

I am the kind of person who finds motivation and passion only when I get connected to something bigger than myself, bigger even than the organization I serve. Coming to work every day with the tepid goal of helping make my organization successful simply doesn't stir my passion. On the other hand, my work becomes both compelling and fulfilling when some daring vision takes me beyond myself, beyond my own personal success, and beyond the organization's success. A compelling vision urges me forward, motivating me to move from where I am to where I'd like to be.

Every effective, energizing vision that I know of grows out of a grand, even breathtaking mission. Such a vision tries to answer the question, "How can we best fulfill our purpose, given our particular circumstances?" In other words, what do we need to become if we want to effectively live out our reason for being? What key target do we need to shoot for? What exalted future do we want to make happen? What new horizon do we want to reach?

Mission and vision work together to define who you are, what you do, how you do it, for whom you do it, and where you want to go in the future. Mission and vision differ from one another, but they absolutely must join forces. If mission is the bow that provides the energy to send an arrow hurtling through the air, then vision is the string that transfers that energy to the arrow. The bow and the string have different functions, but if they don't work together, then the arrow misses the target.

Balanced metrics reveal the resources you use to produce a given state.

Let me illustrate the difference between mission and vision by returning to Christ's Great Commission: "Go into all the world and preach the gospel to all creation." I've called the Great Commission the church's mission, its reason for being. Every Christian church on the planet has the Great

Commission as its mission. That mission doesn't change from place to place or era to era.

Now imagine two local congregations, both equally committed to the Great Commission but located in very different places. Suppose one serves rural Iowa and the other works in inner-city New York. Nearly everything about the context and environment of the Iowa congregation will look vastly different from the one in New York City. Cultural differences, language differences, educational differences, economic differences, historical differences, perspective differences, musical differences—they all add up to *require* that the two dissimilar congregations pursue their identical mission in enormously different ways.

And that's where vision comes in.

Vision gives an organization a blueprint for how it can best fulfill its mission, given its specific circumstances and unique environment. It takes into account an organization's particular setting, its available resources, its current challenges and other distinctive factors, and then dreams of a future in line with its mission that it can bring about through the application of a well-designed strategy.

Maybe the hypothetical Iowa church creates an outreach program designed specifically to help soybean farmers. Would such a program work in inner-city New York? Hardly. On the flip side, perhaps the New York congregation decides to hold seminars for its seniors on navigating the city's mass transit system. Would those seminars attract a crowd in Iowa?

Certainly not. While both endeavors might help their congregations to fulfill their common mission, the unique visions that spawned them would look markedly different from each other.

Vision also differs from mission in that vision can change over a relatively short period, perhaps every few years or once in a decade, while mission changes very little, if at all, over even a very long period. Vision *has* to change in order to address fluctuating external circumstances. So while mission defines an organization's reason for existence—what it's here to do—and therefore remains essentially permanent, vision changes with alterations in external circumstances. Vision pictures some specific direction for the organization that will help it to fulfill its mission within some specified time frame.

Vision Inspires Passion

Early in my professional life, I worked as a college professor, a position I thoroughly enjoyed. I felt quite passionate about teaching, and I took great joy and satisfaction as I saw students learning. At the time, I believed I would spend my whole life teaching college students. I had a clear vision for where my professional life would go.

But times change. Life brings new circumstances. And soon my vision for a lifelong career as a college professor no longer fit the reality of my life. As a person who needs a vital connection to something bigger than myself to keep me motivated and passionate about my work, I had to find or develop a new vision for my life.

Vision and mission should work together to inspire and motivate you toward a strong sense of passion for what you are here on this earth to do. They work hand in hand to supply the key sources of passion that motivate both individuals and organizations.

When I first voiced my vision for Adventist Health System—to become a global pacesetter delivering preeminent, faith-based healthcare—I used the phrase "to become" intentionally. Those two words imply a goal we haven't yet reached, a direction we want to head, a worthy destination that lies ahead of us. Vision can give you and the people in your organization a passion for what they can be in the future. Vision motivates you toward achieving higher goals. It helps you to look beyond the "right now" and toward the "not yet." It gives you a compelling picture of what the future holds for your organization and for the people within it.

Break down resistance to change by giving your people a chance to offer their own ideas for making the new vision work.

I'm an avid reader in large part because of vision. Anybody who knows me recognizes that I work as hard as I can to understand our world. Therefore I don't limit my reading merely to what's going on in the local market of Orlando where our headquarters is located, or in the state of Florida, or even in the United States. I take a global approach to my reading and research, devoting two or three hours every day to surveying the rapidly changing state of healthcare—locally, nationally, and internationally. I do this because I have a passion for our organization's global vision, and because I know how vital it is for me to work from my position as a senior leader to interpret for others the contours of our vision. What does it look like in the context of our mission? Why do we adopt certain strategies to help us pursue that vision?

As hard as you work within your organization to instill passion for your mission statement, so you must labor equally hard to create passion for your vision. You can't simply jot down a vision statement for your organization, pass a memo around the office about it, and expect your people to get out there and make it happen. As a leader, you must pour your heart and soul into developing and defining your vision and into helping the people who work for you to fully understand and passionately embrace what your organization can become.

What Are Your Circumstances?

As you work to develop a vision statement for your organization, you must pay extraordinary attention to the external circumstances that affect your environment. You must take into account the market you'll be serving, your specific location, your financial constraints, the general economic climate, and every other factor that has a significant effect on your organization. But you also must consider how and where you want to lead your organization.

One of the hospitals in our system is located in a small

Appalachian town. It's a facility that provides primary and secondary care, but nothing complicated. Medicare accounts for about 40 percent of its business, with another 40 percent through Medicaid, 6 percent through private insurance, and the rest through charity. The town it is located in has an illiteracy rate of approximately 40 percent, with a high rate of unemployment and a low average income.

Since this small hospital is a part of Adventist Health System, it has the same mission as the largest hospital in our system. They both exist to extend the healing ministry of Christ, but each has a very different vision.

Imagine for a moment that you are the CEO of the small, rural hospital. The challenges you face will look radically different from the ones facing a CEO of one of our large hospitals located in a bustling metropolitan area. You must serve in a difficult market where life is tough, illiteracy is rampant, unemployment is high, average income is low, and where chronic diseases run rampant. You'll have to deal with all of that as you work to provide excellent service in a hospital that lives so close to the financial edge that its management has to closely monitor every dime it spends or takes in.

If mission is the bow that provides the energy to send an arrow hurtling through the air, then vision is the string that transfers that energy to the arrow.

In a situation like that, as the CEO, what would you propose for a vision statement?

You want to develop a vision statement that motivates your employees, that builds off of your mission statement, and that points people to the future in a way that creates passion and excitement. At the same time, you want it to give the good people living in and around your small town confidence that they will receive excellent attention, should they require hospital care. How would you develop that vision statement?

First, you'd thoroughly investigate your context in and around the small town. Once you did that, you would sit down with your administrative colleagues and other leaders to ponder your options. Do you think you'd suggest setting your sights on becoming a global pacesetter in healthcare? Not if you wanted to avoid getting scheduled for an involuntary psychological exam, you wouldn't. No, you simply wouldn't have the resources or the market to accomplish something on such a grand scale.

So what might you suggest as a vision statement for a small community hospital? How could you and your colleagues work to fulfill Adventist Health System's corporate mission? Since you know you have limited resources and you serve a disadvantaged community, perhaps you could set your sights on becoming the finest *rural* hospital in America. Do you think that would make sense? I'd consider that an outstanding vision statement for a hospital operating in Appalachia, the kind that would challenge your hospital's board of directors, administrators, physicians, and others to become great in the setting in which they serve.

Such a vision statement would rule out a lot of worthy initiatives, of course. Your hospital would not, for example, seek to provide more sophisticated medical services than a typical rural hospital usually offers. But it *would* challenge the people who work at your organization to take the hospital's limited portfolio of services and perform them as well or better than the most celebrated non-urban hospital in the country.

In reality, you may never become the CEO of a hospital (large or small). But as in our little exercise, developing a vision for your organization means taking stock of the external circumstances surrounding your organization and then asking yourself how you might accomplish your organization's missional goals in an excellent way, given your circumstances.

As you ponder your organization's current vision, or as you prepare to develop a new one, ask yourself a few questions:

- Who are we serving and in what way?
- What kinds of limitations or advantages do we have in our current situation?
- Given our limitations and advantages, what can we do to perform on a world-class level?
- Is our vision to serve locally, statewide, nationally, or internationally?
- What are our financial constraints?

- What kind of time frame are we considering?
- Do we have the human resources to make our vision a reality?
- Do we serve enough people to justify developing and implementing a new, updated vision?

A vision for your organization's direction doesn't happen on its own, even over a protracted period of time. In fact, disaster usually awaits a leader who stands back and allows his or her organization to go wherever circumstances take it. That's why you as a leader must be intentional and work hard as you develop a vision for what you believe your organization should become.

1. Decide what you will and won't be doing.

Many an organization—for-profit businesses and tax-exempts alike—get themselves in trouble when they overextend themselves by taking on too many tasks. A lack of focus can derail the loftiest of missions and the strongest of visions. In real life, the small Appalachian hospital I mentioned earlier avoided that pitfall by honestly evaluating its external circumstances and concluding that it simply couldn't offer more advanced medical services than its environment could bear. Instead, the hospital focused its work on what it does well: providing basic services.

As a leader working to develop your vision of a world-class organization, begin by focusing on your external circumstances, and then use that analysis to decide what your organization will and won't be doing. This requires real honesty, both with yourself and with your fellow leaders. What do you do well? What causes you to struggle? If, for example, you work in healthcare and you're considering a particular new service, ask yourself, "Do I feel so confident that my facility can provide this new service with such excellence that I would want a close family member to get treated here?" If your answer is "no," then you probably shouldn't attempt to add that service to your organization's healthcare repertoire. Concentrate instead on what you know you can do well.

The best organizations are relentless about weeding out bad processes, systems, and employees.

There's no shame in acknowledging that your external circumstances limit what you can do. In fact, a good leader always knows his limitations. The key is deciding what you'll be taking on and what you won't, and then working hard to provide that service or create that product as well or better than anyone else.

2. Focus your attention on work that will allow you to become truly great.

Mission and vision should always inspire you, your organization, and the people who work for you to keep themselves focused on being the best they can be at whatever they have chosen to do.

Find out what you are truly passionate about doing and then work to be truly great at it. When you focus on what can make you great, you can confidently report to your staff and to the people who work for you, "We know we can do this as well as anyone, anywhere."

3. Look for ways to innovate.

Regardless of the size of your organization, you can continually search for creative ways to provide an increasingly excellent product to your clients and customers. How can you become a more innovative leader? And how can you inspire your staff to become more innovative? How can you find better, more efficient, less costly ways to do what you do well? Every organization has restless people among its ranks—creative men and women who refuse merely to show up every day and do their jobs in exactly the same way as yesterday, especially if they suspect a simple change might provide a big improvement—and you need to search out these people and encourage their creative restlessness. Urge them to find ways to improve your service. And remind them that innovation has a crucial role in good financial stewardship, which enables all of you to better fulfill your mission.

A fresh vision can motivate your organization to charge boldly into the future.

4. Measure/track your growth.

In one sense, developing a new vision for your organization is the same thing as developing a plan for growth. As you work to develop your new vision, find ways to accurately and regularly measure your organization's growth. This will help you to determine what you're doing well, what you're not doing so well, and what concrete steps you can take to make improvements. Tracking helps you to pursue your vision more effectively.

5. Motivate your staff by giving regular reports.

Many world-class organizations make it a point to regularly let their staff know how they're doing. Such communication may come in the form of regular emails, weekly or semiweekly staff meetings, or by providing special reports on a Web site. A mix of metrics (cold, hard numbers outlining revenue, expenditures, and so forth) and anecdotes highlighting upbeat examples of outstanding service can provide excellent motivation for you and your colleagues to pursue your vision and fulfill your mission.

Our organization likes to tell real-life stories about employees who go out of their way to provide what we call "extra-mile service." We've learned that nothing motivates and inspires people to make our vision reality than real-life stories. If you haven't taken advantage of the power of stories, I urge you to give it a try. Organizations that become great almost always have a raft of great stories to tell. And they tell them often and with obvious delight.

Keep the Vision Front and Center

Effective leaders have a way of constantly reiterating the organization's vision so that the vision stays in the forefront of everyone's mind. Human beings need repetition, and so long as that repetition comes in multiple, creative forms, they don't tend to grow weary of it. If a vision is worth pursuing, then it's worth repeating. Remind your people of what they are working toward and what part they are expected to play in it. When people stop thinking about the vision, they usually stop making progress toward it, and that makes it hard to see when problems arise and what adjustments might be necessary.

This need for communication gets kicked up several notches when an old vision gets refurbished or a new vision gets installed. At these times, good leaders really earn their keep. One sure way to bring confusion to an organization (and to damage your status as a leader) is to fail to effectively communicate a new vision.

> *Vision and mission combine to inspire and motivate your passion to fulfill your purpose.*

Most people won't get on board with your vision overnight. It can sometimes take a year or more to fully settle your vision in your people's heads and cement it into their hearts. You must become part salesperson and part teacher. You have to convince your colleagues—sell them on your idea, like a master salesman—that the direction you want to go will benefit them and better equip your organization to fulfill its mission. And you have to teach them and keep on instructing them that you will work with them to grasp where the organization needs to go.

Start this process of communicating organizational vision with your key associates—your board of directors, if you have one, or the other top leaders in your organization. Make sure these influential men and women are fully with you and that they grasp your vision, believe in it, and are in lockstep with you on how to make it happen.

From there, you and your team can begin communicating the vision to others in your organization. This may mean speaking with staff members one-on-one, visiting with key employees in their offices, or finding some other venue to have a helpful discussion. You may need to hold departmental meetings, perhaps even "town-hall" style, where you invite questions and urge people to voice their concerns or offer other kinds of input.

By all means, prepare yourself to answer the tough questions. Significant change can affect your coworkers in myriad and profound ways. Make sure you can explain why your organization needs to start doing things differently and why you believe it must take this new direction.

Overcoming Resistance to Change

Vision has a way of messing with people who don't like change—and most of us would really rather keep things the way they are. Humans are creatures of habit who grow to like and even depend on their habits, both good and bad. New vision always brings change, and change means moving people away from what feels comfortable and safe.

Sometimes, that means you'll have a battle on your hands.

When leaders prepare to make vision-inspired changes in an organization, they can count on several typical responses:

"But we've done it the same way for years!"

"We're doing OK, so why do we need to change anything?"

"Let's not rock the boat."

"We've never done it that way before."

While people don't usually embrace the thought of change, a couple of situations make it far more likely that most will accept or even seek it. The first is what I call "a burning platform of crisis." This occurs when the old ways of doing things no longer work, and everyone with eyes even half open can see it. When the house around you is burning down and you see everything you love going up in smoke, it becomes much easier to say, "Maybe we need to do something different." In such desperate circumstances, employees and associates will often *beg* for change and even offer their own radical suggestions for a new approach.

There is a second circumstance in which people will also accept change. When some compelling vision affects people emotionally, they are also more open to change. When a desirable picture of a new future reaches their heart, when it goes past the cognitive and comes to rest in their wills and longings, then change can become not only desirable but essential.

That's when your job as the leader becomes critical. You must find ways to break through people's natural resistance to change by inspiring and challenging them. You must deftly present a new vision in a way that appeals to your people's passion for their work, that makes them feel comfortable, that doesn't leave them feeling overwhelmed.[3]

You'll get further, faster when you focus on one key fact: Your people are *people*. They each have their own personalities, gifts, fears, and insecurities. Good leaders know that throwing too much change at other human beings too quickly can turn their world chaotic and unstable. The good leader takes all this into consideration when changing an organization.

Vision asks, "How can we best fulfill our purpose, given our particular circumstances?"

No doubt, some decisions must come from the top down. But when a leader makes *all* decisions in that way, it will overwhelm all those who make up the organization and leave them feeling bombarded and abused. When that happens, leaders will almost inevitably face both stiff resistance and a big drop-off in productivity.

You can effectively shepherd in a new vision without overwhelming your people by working hard to engage them in the changes your vision will bring. Remember, you'll be asking your employees to do the work, and they're the ones who have both the knowledge and the experience to offer good input. Everyone tends to perform better when they know their leaders value them and appreciate their input and ideas.

Break down resistance to change by giving your people a chance to offer their own ideas for making the new vision work. That might be as simple as gathering people in groups and saying, "Let's talk about ways that we could improve and build on what we're doing. Does anyone have some ideas that could help us do things better?"

You May Need Sunglasses

Above all, you must communicate with your people, through multiple channels, about what the new vision means and what it can accomplish. Convince them that it makes sense both for them and for their organization. When you do this well, you can achieve dramatic results.

A few years back, a slumping Reuters, one of the world's leading news organizations, recorded losses of almost £500 million. Its CEO described the company as "fighting for survival." But only one year later, the company recorded *profits* of almost £500 million. "Communication was at the heart of this remarkable recovery," wrote a company executive.

As part of its communication strategy to build company-wide support for needed change, Reuters designed and executed a special one-day event that included all its offices in more than 140 countries. The event involved live video feeds,

Q&A sessions, a special website, toolkits, teasers prior to the event, and locally organized social activities after the event. "Feedback from employees both on and following the day was overwhelmingly positive. Even the CEO described it as 'the day the company turned the corner.' "[4]

You may not have the kind of resources available to a global giant like Reuters. And you may not experience the kind of dramatic turnaround that it did. But when you develop a compelling vision consistent with your mission, and when you present that vision in creative ways that show employees how the vision can help both them and their organization to reach new levels of success, then get ready for a bright new day.

You might even need sunglasses.

5

Equipping Your Company for Greater Success

How Metrics Give Meaning to Vision

MANY YEARS AGO, OVER A PERIOD OF ABOUT fifteen awful months, I had to shut down more failing businesses within our corporate family than anybody had ever dreamed of doing. As I began to ponder what we needed to do to make our entire medical system viable again, I couldn't escape the fearful image of a Civil War surgeon. I could see him standing in a tent near the battlefield, blood running off his elbows from all the amputations he had to perform.

I even said to my colleagues, "They're going to start running whenever they see me coming."

That's the terrible task that stared me in the face every day for more than two full years. How many wounded limbs in our vast medical organism would I have to cut off for the body to survive? We had bleeders everywhere, every one of them sucking us dry. We had no choice but to divest ourselves of hospitals and shutter unprofitable subsidiaries, including a travel agency and a drug repackaging company. I enjoyed none of it.

"This isn't what I got excited about doing when I joined this company," I glumly told my colleagues. How had it come to that? We had the right mission. Most of our branches had wonderful vision statements. What had gone so terribly wrong?

Today, I know. In most cases, we lacked adequate metrics to tell us how well (or poorly) we had pursued our vision. We had not subjected the glorious syllables of our vision statements to the hard numbers that would have informed us, long before the blood began to flow, that either radical surgery or the morgue lay directly ahead.

I cannot tell you how happy I feel today that those blood-spattered days of pain and tears ended decades ago. But I will never forget them—and neither will I allow my colleagues to forget them. The stakes are just too high.

Mistaking Indulgence for Compassion

Some leaders of tax-exempt organizations fail to confront poor financial performance or tolerate persistently underachieving coworkers out of what they see as a commitment to "compassion." I believe that too many of them confuse compassion with spineless indulgence.

The failure to confront sloppy business behavior or consistent underperformance is *not* compassionate. Far from it. At the end of the day, it's just cowardice masquerading as kindness. It permits senseless waste to go unchallenged. And all too often, it leads to horrific pain and deep despair of *exactly* the sort that I had to wade through so many years ago.

No employee just starting out in his or her career is going to avoid making mistakes, of course. Some of them will be serious. And all leaders—but especially those serving in tax-exempt, faith-based organizations—*should* exercise love in managing their employees. But real love is never merely indulgent. While it knows how to be tender, it also knows how to be tough. Genuine love never compromises your moral standards. If you think an employee has a lot of potential, then certainly you want to give him or her the chance to right some wrong and so become a good, productive employee. But you don't give that person an *unreasonable* number of chances. The best organizations, whether for-profit or tax-exempt, are relentless about weeding out bad processes, bad systems, and bad employees.

"Vision by the numbers," a component of relentless stewardship, creates a healthy tension in an organization.

Are you?

Let me address an issue common to a specific group of folks: people working at a faith-based organization. Now I realize that many readers of this book do not work at a faith-based organization like I do. That's OK, because the principles I share in this book apply equally well across different kinds of companies with various missions. But no matter the organization, a certain type of approach used by misguided people to mask poor performance or poor stewardship is just wrong. That approach is to misuse a tool or respected source of wisdom to try and justify poor stewardship choices.

In the case of a faith-based organization, what better tool to use than the Bible? Surprisingly, I have seen people use Scripture passages about showing love or compassion or grace to others to try and force an organization—or its leaders—into making poor stewardship decisions.

Now from both a faith and a business perspective, I don't believe the Bible endorses poor stewardship. The idea that it is somehow un-Christian to demand that God's servants wisely use God's resources finds no support in the Scriptures. Jesus began one of his parables like this: "There was a rich man whose manager was accused of wasting his possessions. So he called him in and asked him, 'What is this I hear about you? Give an account of your management, because you cannot be manager any longer' " (Luke 16:1–2). At another time he got even more pointed when answering a question from a follower. Listen to these words from "the gentle Jesus":

> A faithful, sensible servant is one to whom the master can give the responsibility of managing his other household servants and feeding them. If the master returns and finds that the servant has done a good job, there will be a reward. I tell you the truth, the master will

> put that servant in charge of all he owns. But what if the servant thinks, "My master won't be back for a while," and he begins beating the other servants, partying, and getting drunk? The master will return unannounced and unexpected, and he will cut the servant in pieces and banish him with the unfaithful.
>
> And a servant who knows what the master wants, but isn't prepared and doesn't carry out those instructions, will be severely punished. . . . When someone has been given much, much will be required in return; and when someone has been entrusted with much, even more will be required (Luke 12:42–48, NLT).

The apostle Paul insists that "those who have been given a trust must prove faithful" (1 Corinthians 4:2). Now, I see in these passages no reason to give a bad steward a hearty pat on the back, or to turn a blind eye to wasteful, undisciplined managing. Wastefulness and sloppiness are neither moral virtues nor spiritual gifts. In fact, careless waste is wholly incompatible with love. Love insists on taking practical action to help people in need, and to waste a resource means that you no longer have it to use in helping anyone.

A far better way to demonstrate real love is to make sure that you operate effectively, manage your resources efficiently, and earn a reputation as a good steward. Then, out of the surplus you generate through your good stewardship, you will have far more to give to those who need your help the most.

My point is that, no matter what your organization's mission is, you must be careful to not let well-meaning people misuse a source of wisdom (in this case, the Bible) to try and justify poor stewardship of resources. Good stewardship of limited resources is the moral high ground.

And by the way, good stewards keep meticulous records of what they have, how much they spend, what they use, and how much they earn. Today, we would call those "metrics."

Are Metrics Evil?

Why do so many employees of tax-exempt organizations seem to shy away from metrics? Why do they so dislike numbers-based indicators that measure their effectiveness? I've heard many of them speak of metrics almost as the enemy of mission and vision. Why?

Business people in the for-profit world expect to get measured continuously. They know their superiors will hold them accountable to a specified set of metrics. But over and over again in the tax-exempt world, I've seen good people—gripped by the power of a great mission and motivated by the glory of a grand vision—refuse to make themselves accountable to hard measures of success.

Please, take it from someone who once felt like a Civil War surgeon: metrics are not evil, nor are they the enemy of mission and vision. In fact, those very metrics have the power to equip you for success. Ignoring them will almost certainly lead to your failure. As a leader, you *must* find a way to measure your organization's success that is concrete, real, easy to define, easy to understand, and that supports the vision you've worked so hard to develop and communicate. Organizations that establish and achieve such metrics have an astronomically better chance of reaching their vision than those who do not. Your vision must be both quantifiable and measurable.

At all the hospitals in our system, unless the vision is quantifiable, it's just talk. Earlier I mentioned the "five pillars" that our Florida hospitals use to judge performance (finance, quality and safety, service, market, and team). In all five of those pillars, we insist on establishing several concrete metrics that measure critical values related to the specific pillar. Part of our vision calls for us to be in the top decile of all five pillars. If we manage that—and the numbers will tell us if we do—then we can claim to be a global pacesetter in modern healthcare.

> *Before you try out any new vision statement, make sure you know how to measure your success.*

You must identify several appropriate "pillars" for your own organization, and then establish and use adequate metrics that will tell you, with precision, whether you're successfully pursuing your vision.

Why Metrics Matter

Metrics give meaning to your vision. They also safeguard its health. And if you want your organization to thrive, you absolutely need them. Allow me to suggest three reasons why every great vision needs to partner with appropriate, robust metrics.

1. Good metrics keep you in touch with reality.

Leaders who lack discipline, who dislike the idea of making themselves and their organizations accountable to hard measures of success, often become delusional. They live out of touch with reality, which I consider to be the single most dangerous threat to any group or individual. Self-delusion, kidding yourself about your true circumstances, can kill you. That's why I think of it as the most dangerous threat to an organization's health.

No one can escape (or *should* be able to escape) the accountability of solid finances. Financial metrics are simply a way of measuring how you use resources and whether you use them wisely or unwisely. The numbers will tell you whether you are a good steward or a bad steward.

You need metrics that measure more than finances, however. In our industry, we need metrics on everything from patient experience to staff satisfaction, from safety concerns to market share. Metrics in each of these critical areas help to keep us from descending into self-delusion.

What are the critical areas in your own organization?

Where would numerical measures of your performance help to keep you from crashing into self-delusion?

2. The proper use of appropriate metrics can provide great motivation.

Having a balanced set of metrics (see chapter 3) can be highly motivational, because those numbers can clearly tell you whether you're *really* fulfilling your mission and *effectively* pursuing your vision. Why? Because they're intimately tied to what you're all about. You've identified these specific metrics because they tie directly to your mission and vision, to the very things that grab at your heart and the hearts of your employees.

If I were directing a department, let's say in food service, I would think, *What should I do to make sure my department lines up with our corporate mission? How will I know if I'm on track? What are the key numbers that will tell me if we're headed in the right direction? What core metrics will ring loud bells if we start going off course?*

I look at it this way: If our mission is right and our vision is right, then we're doing the work of the angels—and that means we ought to do this better than anyone. If I tolerate bad procedures and bad systems, then I'm going to wash good resources right down the drain. And when I allow that to happen, I will serve fewer people than I could have, or I will serve them far more poorly than I could have. Good metrics motivate me to serve the largest number of people I can manage with the best service I can deliver. The wise use of our limited resources motivates me, because it translates into us being able to better serve a larger number of needy people. Metrics, used wisely, provide us with highly positive motivation to do our jobs well.

3. Paying attention to good metrics can keep you from poor quality, which is inherently expensive.

Almost always, appropriately using metrics produces superior financial outcomes. World-class organizations understand that poor quality is inherently more expensive. Good metrics help you to weed out the flawed processes that cause inefficiencies and waste. And neglecting to develop those metrics, and use them properly, will lead to serious consequences for your entire organization. Mess-ups and sloppiness are hugely expensive. When you waste too many resources, invariably you get to the place where you can't do what you really want to do simply because you won't have the resources to do it.

Your most critical task is to influence those who report directly to you.

Regardless of their inspiring vision statements, tax-exempt organizations can go bankrupt just as certainly as for-profits can. It happens all the time. I know of many tax-exempt healthcare systems that defaulted on their bond payments, which amounts to the same thing as insolvency. When you can no longer pay your bills, you go out of business, regardless of your noble mission or your rousing vision statement.

A few years ago, a headline blared, "Bad credit news for non-profit hospitals continues."[5] The accompanying article described how an unwise dependence on "junk bonds" had threatened the very existence of a number of small, tax-exempt hospitals. "The net result of all of this isn't just hospital CFOs with migraines," the article said, "it's also falling ratings on hospital debt." The article concluded, "As ratings agencies like Moody's and Standard & Poor's continue to lower ratings on hospital debt, there could very well be a cascade of hospitals defaulting in the first or second quarter of next year."

Do not confuse compassion with spineless indulgence.

The news hasn't improved much since then. Not long ago, another headline declared, "Small, nonprofit hospitals struggle."[6] This article reported that Moody's downgraded its already shaky rating of a 138-bed tax-exempt hospital with five hundred employees. The hospital had $25.7 million in outstanding bonds and an unfunded pension liability of $17.6 million, up from $6.5 million the previous year.

That hospital has lots of (worried) company. At the time of this book's writing, Moody's had recently downgraded a record $20 *billion* in tax-exempt hospital debt.[7] And Reuters reported that Moody's was about to downgrade another five tax-exempt, small hospitals.[8]

Now I can't claim that the affected hospitals all suffer from inadequate metrics, which led to poor quality, which caused a sharp rise in their operating expenses. Maybe none of them have such a problem. Maybe if I were leading them, they'd all be in worse shape than they are now. I don't know. But I *do* know that a failure to use good metrics has caused many other hospitals before them to follow a similar track into bankruptcy or forced sale. And I also know that good metrics can help you to avoid poor quality, which is inherently expensive (and not infrequently, fatal).

Bad Habits as a Result of Poor Metrics

Again, numbers are simply a way to measure health. It's hard to argue with accurate numbers, whether you're in a for-profit or a tax-exempt corporation. All organizations struggle when they fall into either of two bad habits.

1. Lack of good tools.

Some organizations simply don't have the right tools to measure the right things. Because of that, they can't even get at some of the information they desperately need. They've never built or acquired the good measurement tools that could help them to ascertain how they're doing.

In 1985 Motorola designed a set of tools, eventually called Six Sigma, intended to improve its manufacturing processes. The company wanted to figure out how to drive out all variation apart from common cause variation, which no one can eliminate. Ten years later, Jack Welch at General Electric adopted Six Sigma, making it famous. Today, companies in a wide variety of industries around the world use Six Sigma (sometimes called Lean Six Sigma) to improve the quality of their processes by minimizing unwanted variability in the manufacture of products and the implementation of processes. The name, Six Sigma, comes from the statistical modeling terms used in the manufacturing process. A "sigma rating" indicates the percentage of defect-free products that a specified manufacturing process generates. The higher the rating, the fewer the defects per million.

Six Sigma reflects the attitude, "We're going to relentlessly seek to drive out anything wasteful." I think tax-exempt organizations (and yes, especially faith-based ones) ought to embrace such an attitude with everything in them. Given our missions and visions, why should anyone out there be better stewards than us?

Six Sigma is not the only quality measurement tool available, of course. But it is one of the most tried, tested, and respected. (Six Sigma training and certification is widely available through a number of organizations and schools. Courses are generally available both online and in person.)

2. Failure to use correctly the good tools already in hand.

Some organizations have the right tools that are designed to inform the metrics, but their leaders don't pay enough attention to them. Or they have the right tools, but they focus in such an unbalanced way on a single metric that they make that lone indicator the *summum bonum* of the entire organization. And so they ignore all the others. In other words, they make a single dimension of performance equal to their whole mission; and inevitably, they get so unbalanced that at some point they can no longer pursue their vision.

I insist that our leaders keep what I call a "balanced scorecard." In our industry, such a scorecard considers: good clinical outcomes, safe clinical processes, caring about the patient's service experience, sound finances, and even (in our case) how well we're meeting a patient's spiritual needs. We want to create a relentless atmosphere that expresses the love of the Creator for each person who comes through our doors. In today's environment, I can see no valid excuses for failing to have a balanced scorecard. Every mission-driven organization needs a board of directors and a team of competent managers who are fully committed to a balanced scorecard, one with good metrics that measure the right things. Equally important is a firm commitment to hold everyone in the organization accountable for meeting those metrics.

Vision can give people a passion for what they can be in the future.

It makes me happy that advances in automation have enabled us to measure our clinical care processes and our outcomes, both collectively and individually, in a way never possible before. I consider that a fabulous thing.

A Healthy Tension

Although doing "vision by the numbers" creates tension in an organization, it's a healthy tension. If you as a leader institute some "lean thinking" or adopt some Six Sigma–like process, your actions will produce tension, because that kind of thinking and those kinds of processes force people to constantly look at what they're doing. But while it creates a certain tension, it also prompts positive change within the organization, which enables you to more effectively pursue your vision.

Good metrics can keep you from poor quality, which is inherently expensive.

I call it a healthy tension, in part, because the use of metrics judges processes and products, not an individual's personal performance. It gives you a meaningful way of measuring your processes and their outcomes; and frankly, people quickly learn to respect it.

The clinicians I work with understand that our organization uses metrics out of a desire to reduce to the absolute minimum the chance of a serious injury to a patient—maybe administering the wrong drug, or giving a dangerous dose of the right drug. This challenges our clinicians at the very core of the reason that they became caregivers in the first place: They want to take good care of their patients. So even though the use of metrics produces tension, it's a positive tension. And you need to be relentless about it.

Defeating Two Big Enemies

I didn't come to healthcare with a marketing background or even a traditional business or finance background. I came as a scientist. And so I love thinking about information and what it means.

More than twenty years ago, the lack of metrics in healthcare really bothered me. I heard about some measurement processes a healthcare system out West had been using, so I called them up one day and asked, "May I come out there to see what you're doing?" What I observed answered some of my troubling questions, and as a result, I identified two main enemies of quality and cost regarding the way our own organization operated.

1. Waste generated by physicians lacking up-to-date data on best practices.

Orders by physicians not based on the most up-to-date scientific evidence regarding how best to treat a particular condition caused a great deal of waste. Today, because physicians more often give order sets based on evidence related to best practice, the waste has declined significantly. We've begun to publish our findings on the improvements we've seen, and we'll publish more shortly, some of it in collaboration with Johns Hopkins. Good baselines in our accounting already have revealed dramatic reductions in cost regarding certain kinds of testing, in the use of antibiotics, and for excessive length of stay. We've plotted the costs when we use evidence-based sets and when we don't, and the difference is striking.

2. Waste generated by lack of coordination between hospital disciplines.

We are now working throughout our system to develop ideal interdisciplinary plans of care, again based on scientific evidence. Theoretically, if we had the perfect order sets and each clinical team implemented those order sets according to the best current thinking in each discipline, we should be able to eliminate a great deal of waste. Our goal is to make the whole process as frictionless and smooth as possible.

Think of your organization as a single ecosystem. Everything in the organization is interconnected with everything else. If you can help your various departments to more efficiently work together, you'll see significant cost savings in a fairly short period of time.

If our pharmacy receives a physician's orders and then thinks about everything it can do in an interdisciplinary way so that it doesn't act as though it operates in a silo, someone might well imagine a better way to interact with their colleagues in other parts of the hospital.

If the nursing staff begins thinking in the same way, someone there might get a great idea about how to improve their interaction with the pharmacy. And if we in administration ponder how we might use technology to better support our nurses, we might see how to take certain rote processes off their backs as much as possible, or figure out how to reduce the amount of time they have to spend doing documentation. If every discipline, taking into account the interdisciplinary nature of patient care, does the same thing, I expect to find vast opportunities for improvements in processes and reductions in cost.

A good vision statement pictures an attainable future that motivates people to reach for some attractive scenario a significant distance beyond their current grasp.

A few years ago, the Rand Corporation did a study to get a feel for what inpatient inefficiencies cost the US healthcare system each year; the estimate came in at close to a *trillion* dollars. And that study didn't even consider the coordination between physicians in a non-hospital setting, or coordinating interdisciplinary care, or encouraging better health habits, or a hundred other possibilities. Every bit of that equation represents an immense opportunity to do better at lower cost.

I love the task of educating, so whenever I get the chance, I tell employees, "In this journey of constant improvement, whether in regard to processes, science, best practice, or any other tool, we're really after just one thing: a safer, more effective experience for our patients."

I fully expect the benefits to rain down.

Metrics That Help Substitute Gain for Loss

One of our physicians, a respected leader in his department, once informed me (with more than a little anger) that several of his colleagues were doing a number of invasive procedures . . . and doing them poorly. Not only did these unnecessary procedures cause a lot of waste, he said, but they also subjected many patients to needless and even dangerous risk. The hospital ended up having to fix a lot of serious problems that never would have occurred had these procedures not happened in the first place.

We spent four or five years developing evidence-based metrics to address the problem and eliminate it. At the end of that time, we produced a peer-reviewed standard that everyone regarded as fair and absolutely unchallengeable. Those metrics both reduced our costs and significantly improved patient safety. Also, because of those metrics, approximately ten physicians either lost their authorization to conduct such procedures or left our staff altogether. The result? The safety and quality of that department shot up dramatically.

Anytime you have to fix some mistake—in our case, whether an infection that never should have occurred because you incorrectly managed a central line, or some other foolish error—you have to fix the gaffe at great cost. That's a pure waste. It's loss to the patient and it's loss to the organization. However you look at it, it's loss.

The more accurate and robust metrics that you bring to the table, therefore, the more you ensure that your organization effectively pursues your vision. The more that happens, the less loss you will see.

And isn't that a huge gain for everyone?

6

When It's Time for Your Vision to Change

What to Do So You Don't Settle for Average

NEARLY EVERYWHERE I'VE LANDED professionally, I've had to refresh or change the vision statement of the organization I came to lead. That doesn't mean I always found something desperately wrong with the new group; sometimes I found something very, very right.

When I took the reins at one high-performing organization, for example, I found that while it had some excellent strategic plans, it had no specific vision statement. The group's excellent leaders could tell me, "These are our goals and we intend to achieve this next level of metric," but they had no compelling picture of the organization's future, nothing that really stirred the blood of their coworkers and got them passionate for pursuing a new level of excellence and service.

Had these leaders been students of mine during my years as a college professor, I might have thought, *These kids have a solid B average and want to get a B+, but they don't realize they have the ability to make the Dean's List and maybe even get a perfect 4.0 grade point average.* The people in this strong organization needed a more radical vision of their future, something with the power to capture the imagination of the whole group and drive it forward to explore an exciting place they hadn't yet even dreamed of visiting.

Notice, however, that I began this chapter with the word *nearly*. Just because you ride into town on your white stallion doesn't mean you have to say, "OK, par'ners, listen up. There's a new sheriff in town, and things are a-gonna change around here, right quick." In fact, you may inherit a situation in which the vision statement already in place fits *exactly* the needs and challenges of the moment. Why go to all the work of changing an organization's vision when you don't have to? And make no mistake, it takes *a lot* of time, effort, and imagination to successfully incorporate a new vision into an existing organization's culture.

So then—when do you know the time has come to make a change in the vision of the organization you lead? Under what circumstances and in what kind of environment does it make sense to initiate such a big change in direction? I can think of at least three primary situations in which a change in vision becomes highly beneficial, if not necessary, if the organization is to thrive.

It's Time to Change When . . .

Both bad conditions and great circumstances can serve as the catalyst for changing an organization's vision. A struggling organization usually requires a change in vision, while a booming one may need a new vision to challenge it to reach even greater heights. And both struggling and thriving groups may need a new vision when major changes in the environment loom on the horizon. You know that the time for seriously considering a change in your organization's vision and vision statement has come when . . .

1. You inherit an unhealthy culture.

When a new leader comes into an organization and perceives something decidedly unhealthy there, that leader may have little choice but to make significant changes. Very often, it's that unhealthy culture that brought the new leader to the organization in the first place. The powers that be recognized that unless some big shifts occurred, the organization could not survive.

Every time I've taken a new job in healthcare, I've made it a habit to spend a significant amount of time assessing the situation before making any major changes. But after I've made that assessment, I've sometimes said, "You know, the way we relate to our patients and how we communicate with them just doesn't work. We are going to do something about that." I've then spent concentrated time trying to craft a potent vision statement that pictured what kind of an organization we were going to become. And in every case, those new vision statements played an enormous role in generating major shifts in our organizational culture.

Suppose you inherit a situation in which your coworkers have grown lax in their job performance. Across the board, you see that they lack any real accountability for how they pursue their assigned tasks. Good people have been allowed to get by with, at best, mediocre performance. And yet to many, the very idea of holding anyone accountable to some kind of fair and evidence-based metrics has become unthinkable.

Metrics give meaning to your vision and safeguard its health.

Remember that while some people seem determined to remain mediocre, the vast majority want nothing to do with mediocrity. They *want* to be challenged, grow, develop, and become good at what they do. They *want* to feel proud of what they're accomplishing. And so to help them reach that new, challenging plateau, you consciously tap into the power of your organizational mission to create a new vision that they can believe in and then passionately pursue.

In the case of deep dysfunction, you must get to work quickly; you simply don't have the luxury of slight modifications to diet, coupled with six months' bed rest. Your patient will die without radical surgery and a complete lifestyle change. This is the kind of situation I faced early in my healthcare career when I envisioned myself as a Civil War surgeon, blood dripping off my elbows from all the corporate amputations I had to perform. I couldn't wait around to convince people we had to make some significant changes. We either changed or died. So, despite the excruciating pain, we made those changes. And that's why we're still around today, looking forward to the bright future we see ahead of us.

2. You face a major shift in your environment.

A vision statement is a high-level strategic roadmap of where you want to be somewhere down the road, maybe five or ten years into the future. Now suppose that, as you look ahead, you see several significant changes coming to your industry, to your geographical region, or to your larger environment. Usually, you will have to change your organization's vision and vision statement in response to these changes, because if you don't, the major shifts thundering toward your industry or environment will bury you.

In my world, the Affordable Care Act represented exactly that kind of major shift in environment. It brought into play new ways that hospitals must work with doctors as a part of attacking the spiraling costs of healthcare. A second big environmental change in our industry concerned what I call the collapse of the private practice of medicine. For three decades, as I served in various leadership roles in the healthcare industry, we watched this situation unfold. Almost nothing that once existed in the typical community hospital environment still exists today. Hospitals have had no choice but to find totally new ways to work with physicians. If a system like ours refuses to deal with the situation and fails to make ear-catching statements to prompt new thinking throughout the institution, then it *will* get clobbered. The coming changes *will* run over it.

The vision statements now in place in Adventist Health System clearly reflect these new environmental developments. But until recent years, while we had developed strategic plans for addressing regional healthcare concerns, we had nothing visionary that declared, "We must get ready for national healthcare reform and for the radical changes coming to our environment because of the death of private medical practice." Our vision statements exist today because of these realities; in fact, we developed them for that specific purpose.

Every industry and organization must respond to significant environmental changes. Earlier, I described a hypothetical scenario involving two churches, one in rural Iowa and another in inner-city New York. Now let's consider a different church-related scenario. Let's say you pastor a church that has served the same community for several decades. Over the past ten years or so, you've seen your community change in many significant ways. It used to be largely rural; now it's mostly suburban. Where once your community had a preponderance of older people—empty-nesters, retirees, and elderly men and women—now you see a huge influx of young families, singles, and young professionals. Here's the point: If you grasp at *all* the changing dynamics of your neighborhood, then you had better start considering how to significantly alter your vision so you can effectively fulfill your unchanging mission. Your failure to do so will quickly make you and your ministry irrelevant.

An acquaintance of mine recently told me about a conversation he had with the pastor of an inner-city church in a major metropolitan area in the Pacific Northwest. That pastor has served his congregation faithfully for twenty-five years, and during that time the church has seen some significant growth. But lately that pastor has fielded several anguished telephone calls from the pastors of many other inner-city congregations in his city. They all have the same kinds of questions, centering around the phenomenon of gentrification.

Your organization is an ecosystem; everything is interconnected with everything else.

"Pastor," they'll say, "we have waves of young, white, single professional people coming to our church. What do I do with them? They don't fit our culture. They don't think like we do. But they seem to like worshiping with us. What should we do?"

It sounds to me as though the time has come for a new vision, summarized in a fresh, potent vision statement.

3. Your organization needs a new challenge.

Long before I arrived as president and CEO at Florida Hospital, the organization had evolved into something noteworthy, due mostly to its outstanding leadership. As I looked around, however, I came to believe that the time had come for the people in the organization to collectively lift their eyes, gaze out at the horizon, and raise their expectations of what they could be. Soon I started talking about becoming a national and even international pacesetter in delivering preeminent, faith-based healthcare. I wanted to raise the organization's vision beyond being an outstanding regional hospital and get our people saying, "We will have national and even international significance. We will deliver preeminent healthcare."

Almost immediately, some individuals had a question for me. "What do you mean by 'preeminent?' " they wondered. I replied with the definition, "In the first rank." I didn't mean to say that we intended to become better than anybody else in the world, but that we intended to be in the first rank of the organizations generally seen as international pacesetters.

Why did we make this change? As I saw how much the organization had been blessed, it almost felt like an obligation. The right ingredients had been assembled for something special to happen, and it didn't seem right to shoot for anything less. The organization had grown to the point where it needed a new, aggressive vision.

Try to think back to your ten-year-old self. What dreams did you have for your future? Very likely, those dreams looked very different from the ones that captured your heart at age twenty-one. Why? Because you had grown from a kid into a young adult. You had mastered new skills and felt drawn to greater opportunities. Your ten-year-old dreams of working as an ice cream truck driver perhaps morphed into a desire to become president of an internationally famous dairy conglomerate. But however your dreams changed, they reflected a more mature, knowledgeable, competent, and visionary *you.*

The same principle holds true for organizations. If you become the leader of an organization on the cusp of international frozen confection greatness, then don't settle for finding a better tune to play on your neighborhood ice cream trucks.

How Do You Change the Vision?

Even when you know the time has come for a change, the question still remains: *How do I accomplish it? How do I get it done?* Most people don't like change, and a change in vision seems especially troublesome to many. If you walk into a situation where the mantra "We've always done it this way" rules, then you have to be especially careful about how you proceed. Old-timers may well respond to your new vision with skepticism or even outright resistance. So how do you go about instituting your new vision?

> *Genuine love for others never compromises your moral standards.*

1. Understand that such a big change takes time to take root.

None of this happens quickly, because none of it is easy. The process of instituting a new organizational vision can present formidable challenges, even for the most seasoned leader, and particularly if the organization has an unhealthy corporate culture. As a general rule of thumb, it can take up to five years to reset a culture so that it won't revert to its former self. People just don't change that easily.

Even at Florida Hospital, where I found a healthy culture and a motivated workforce, it took a significant period of time and a lot of discussion before people really bought in to the new vision statement. It took awhile before many of our folks even felt sure they knew what I meant. It probably took nine to twelve months before the majority began to say, "Oh, now I see. Yes. I can support that." And interestingly enough, most of that progress occurred in response to discussions of metrics and how they would help to define both "preeminent" and "global pacesetting."

When you get ready to bring a new vision to your organization, remember that adapting an old vision or instituting a new one usually means you're in for a long process. It simply doesn't happen overnight.

2. Get your leaders on board.

Some of your director-level people will be with you almost from Day One. They've been waiting for something like this, and likely they would have left if something like it hadn't happened. They're ready to move, which makes them great assets for you. You can continually point to them and highlight what they or their departments are doing. Usually these are high performers who won't wait around long once they think some necessary changes need to happen. Competent, highly motivated people usually get frustrated if the leader doesn't take significant steps to fix an unhealthy environment.

Other important leaders in your organization won't take to the changes quite as quickly, however. For them, you'll have to put the vision out there and then get ready to answer a barrage of questions. Some of these questions you can predict, almost like clockwork. Others will come out of left field. Remain patient, have good answers ready, and marshal your best energies at getting these leaders on the same page with you. If you can manage this, you've nearly won the war.

3. Talk about it constantly.

Don't mimic the foolish husband who told his wife, "I told you at our wedding that I loved you, and I shouldn't have to repeat myself unless things change." People need to hear the new vision, over and over again, in multiple ways and in many contexts. Think of it as a new language that your coworkers need to master. They don't know the new vocabulary, the new syntax, or the new grammar. And the only way they'll get fluent in this new language is to hear it constantly from a native speaker. That would be you.

Talk constantly about the new vision. Write about it in newsletters and memos. Mention it in the lunchroom. Emphasize it in strategy sessions. Bring it up in every meeting and every departmental session. You simply can't discuss it enough.

4. Make changes in personnel, if necessary.

If you find one or two among your senior management staff who resist the changes, and things don't substantially improve after a few months, then you'll have to ask these individuals to move on. You need some new blood eager to use their influence to incorporate the new vision into your organizational DNA. If my experience provides any guidance, part of the equation almost always involves some amount of personnel change.

Below the leadership level, you will find some individuals in your organization who feel determined to "ride it out." They hope the changes won't take root and that eventually the former climate will return. After a period of time, when at last they recognize that the new vision (and everything that goes along with it) is not going away, many will start to leave. They may even tell you they're trying to find the kind of place that you just destroyed.

> *Don't let your vision outstrip your organization's potential.*

Thank them, and then let them go.

5. Reinforce the vision with every decision you make.

Speak the vision constantly, and then consistently live it out. Reinforce the new vision with every decision you make, with who you reward, and by choosing carefully who in the organization you make into a hero. Recognize and praise vision-consistent behavior, not to embarrass anyone, but to encourage everyone.

The opposite is equally true. You may have some influential employees or leaders who have real trouble accepting the new vision. Your silence about them can speak like a megaphone. Most people are quite observant, and they will quickly notice who you are *not* praising and complimenting . . . and it won't take them long to make the connection. Without saying a word, you can influence observers to get on board with your company's new direction.

Pitfalls to Avoid When Changing the Vision

You already know that a change in vision takes time to accomplish, so I know you won't make the rookie mistake of trying, practically overnight, to force a new vision on an established organization. Right? But there are a couple of other mistakes that many leaders commonly make, and by so doing make their jobs far harder than they need to be.

1. Avoid the impression that you're unfair or impatient.

When you come in as the leader, strive to show everyone, from the very beginning, that you will deal with one and all in a fair and patient way. Work hard to clearly state the new vision and show in practical terms why the organization needs to change. But then work just as hard to demonstrate that you're patient enough to give people a fair chance to change and move with the new vision. If you fail to give people this chance, then almost certainly you'll be seen as rash and capricious, someone who perhaps should not be in the top spot. I've seen more than one leader flame out due in large part to a lack of both patience and fairness.

Give your people a chance to change, and only if they refuse to do so (after some reasonable length of time), should you require them to move on. Still, fairness doesn't mean indulgence, and patience doesn't mean forever. If you learn the difference, you will do well.

2. Try never to reverse course.

Leaders sometimes ask me, "What happens if you set a strong vision for your organization, but it doesn't work out? What if you set your sights too high?" Maybe you became the leader of a small, rural hospital and you led the charge to become the best performing rural hospital in the world; but three years down the road, you realized you shot too high. Your metrics look poor and it appears that you need to reinvent your vision, because it has begun to demotivate your people rather than embolden them. You've started to hear them whisper, "Oh, we're never going to get there. We're finished."

I have but one main piece of counsel for you here: *Don't let your vision outstrip your organization's potential.* At all costs, avoid shooting from the hip. Don't be too quick to decide on a new vision. Don't even think of floating one until you've been around for a while, seen what goes on, and understood the challenges and context of the organization. If you were the leader of that rural hospital, perhaps you might have better served your organization by developing a vision that said, "No rural hospital in our state will be better than us."

And before you try out *any* vision statement, make sure that you know how you plan to measure your success. What are the key metrics? If you don't know the answer to that question, then keep quiet until you do know.

I frankly don't know how you "back up" from an inappropriate vision statement. Backing up can discourage, demoralize, and even devastate an already unstable organization or shaky department. A good vision statement pictures an *attainable* future that motivates people to reach for some attractive scenario several miles ahead of them. It won't have them reaching for the stars if they have yet to learn how to jump.

An Example of How We Changed Our Vision

Let's take a look at how a change in vision made a difference by examining how Adventist Health System made just such a change. In some ways, I believe the transformation we underwent—and continue to undergo—represents the confluence of all three of the major "reasons to change your vision" considered in this chapter.

Let's begin by taking a snapshot of our industry (which is something I highly recommend you do for your own industry).

Recently I returned from a meeting in which representatives of every healthcare system in attendance talked incessantly about wellness. They weren't merely saying, "This will be a nice, value-added little thing for our patients," but rather, "We're facing all kinds of new risk, and we won't survive if we don't find a way to make our populations healthier."

Maybe you've heard radio spots or seen TV discussions about the changes coming to consumer health insurance programs. Someone told me the other day about a large grocery store chain that announced it is considering graduated health insurance premiums for its workers, based on how much the worker weighs, the individual's blood pressure numbers, or his/her exercise habits, etc. Along the same lines, I'm hearing healthcare system leaders saying, "We need the consumer to get some skin in the game, too, or we might not make it."

Instituting a new organizational vision can present formidable challenges, even for the most seasoned leader.

I can't help but grin as I overhear such discussions, because the pioneers of the Adventist movement began focusing on "health as a lifestyle" more than a century and a half ago. Battle Creek, Michigan—where many of our "original" nurses and physicians trained—even became known as Health City.

In recent years, we built on their work by developing what we call CREATION Health, which focuses on eight principles for fostering total person wellness, based on timeless insights drawn from the biblical book of Genesis. The eight principles are Choice, Rest, Environment, Activity, Trust, Interpersonal, Outlook, and Nutrition (hence, the acronym CREATION; see www.CREATIONHealth.com for further information). We've seen this approach help patients for many years, but not until fairly recently did we start to connect CREATION Health with what's happening nationally in healthcare. I and a few of my colleagues recognized that it might well become a critical part of our economic survival in the emerging healthcare environment.

A few years ago, we instructed every hospital in our system to look for ways to create new business opportunities using these eight lifestyle principles, as well as finding innovative ways to incorporate them into our existing business processes. Many exciting new initiatives have emerged. Perhaps most important, we've seen our thinking transformed. We've moved from giving lip service to the idea—"Well, of course, we want people to be healthy and well"—to actually saying, "OK, how are we going to make this happen? What are we going to do as an organization?" We have directed major financial and intellectual resources toward "making this happen."

As a result, we have seen the emergence of a strong desire to create a culture of health in churches and businesses. Even before the new national healthcare environment began making everyone nervous, we had an interest in connecting with such populations; but not until we made it part of our vision did we see any strong movement in that direction. Certain groups within our organization now focus exclusively on helping churches and businesses to get healthy, including organizations that lack an explicit faith component. But even these groups have noted the healthcare challenges ahead and have said to us, "We see the clear value of whole-person health, and we'd like to jump on board."

In some ways, what we see happening around our CREATION Health program represents the confluence of all three of the major "reasons to change your vision" considered in this chapter. First, the healthcare system in this country has been "sick" for a long time, and major changes are long overdue. Second, the national healthcare environment in the United States is about to change in a massive and irrevocable way, and we must do everything we can to get prepared for it. And third, our CREATION Health initiatives seem tailor-made to address the current national obsession about wellness; now we need, as a system, to step up to the daunting challenge of making it available to the millions of patients who need it.

> *Disaster usually awaits any leader who stands back and allows an organization to go wherever circumstances take it.*

The Future of Your Organization

If you lead an organization that has developed an unhealthy

culture; if you work in an industry or region facing challenges that threaten to alter your corporate environment; or, if you lead a group that has performed so well that you need to lift everyone's eyes to new, bigger, and exciting challenges—then it may be time for a new vision. You must think hard about designing and presenting a blueprint of the future for your organization with the power to inspire your people to become all they can be.

It won't all happen overnight. But if you work patiently to weave it into the fabric of your culture, then you may well end up with an organizational fabric so luxurious and fine that observers will wonder what you did to get it. And best of all, perhaps you'll accompany your people on one of the best trips of all time—the "Road to Fulfillment." You're sure to witness marvelous sights along the way, and all because you have the vision to really *see*.

SECTION SUMMARY

TWELVE TIPS ON HOW VISION DRIVES SUCCESS

1. Vision is critical. Disaster usually awaits any leader who stands back and allows an organization to go wherever circumstances take it.

2. A fresh vision can give people a passion for what they can be in the future.

3. A good vision statement pictures an attainable future that motivates people to reach for some attractive scenario a significant distance beyond their current grasp.

4. Before you try out any new vision statement, make sure you know how to measure your success.

5. Effective leaders constantly reiterate the organizational vision so that it stays in the forefront of everyone's mind.

6. While it may seem obvious, use your vision to focus on work that will allow your organization to become truly great.

7. New vision always brings change, and change means moving people away from what feels comfortable and safe. Expect resistance, but break it down by giving people a chance to offer their own ideas for making the new vision work.

8. The best organizations are relentless about weeding out bad processes, systems, and employees.

9. An organization's vision must change in response to significant alterations in external circumstances.

10. A lack of focus can derail the loftiest of missions and the strongest of visions.

11. Make sure you have adequate metrics to indicate how well or poorly you are pursuing your vision.

12. Good stewardship of limited resources is the moral high ground.

KEY THREE

CRITICAL VALUES

If you think of vision and mission as an organization's head and heart, then the values it holds are its soul.

— Buzzotta/Lefton/Cheney/Beatty,
Making Common Sense Common Practice

In This Section You Will:

- Discover why your organization's values are its corporate "soul."
- Understand how your corporate values are the ambassadors of your organization.
- Discover three ways that a leader can foster values-directed behavior in his or her organization.
- See how corporate values can serve as "guardrails" to keep your organization safely en route to the fulfillment of your mission.
- Learn how relentless stewardship and excellent performance will serve your mission well in any climate.

7

Behavior Must Match Words

The Critical Place of Values

I DOUBT THAT ANY INDIVIDUAL OR GROUP CAN become world class without a strong sense of values.

In the world of sports, athletes become world class not just through their natural ability but because they embrace and practice values such as hard work, healthy lifestyle, and dedication to the specific skills associated with their sport. Only then can they become the best on the planet.

Values shape and mold organizations, businesses, and even countries every bit as much as they equip athletes to become world class. Show me an organization that lacks either a well-defined list of values or doesn't bother to make those values a key part of its culture, and I will show you an organization destined for mediocrity.

Show me an organization with a strong sense of its values and a corresponding and unbending commitment to live out those values, and I'll smile and think, *Now, **that's** an organization laying the groundwork for growing into something truly world class.*

If you're not interested in your organization becoming world class, then ignore your values. But if becoming world class appeals to you, then make sure you—and your people—know what your organizational values are and how they shape and color everything you do. And remember this: If you as the leader neglect your values and you don't emphasize living those values to your organization, then no one else will give them a second thought.

What Are Values?

What is an organizational value? How does it function? What does it do for an organization? What difference does it make if the members of an organization know and live out the stated values of their organization?

Here's my thumbnail definition of values: A code that informs and shapes your daily behavior. Values are much more than ideals to which you give mental assent. They are a carefully chosen collection of behavioral norms that describe how you want to operate, interact with people, make decisions, and conduct yourself, both in public and in private.

Your *personal* values influence how you behave, how you treat others, how you think, and how you speak. They are at the heart of who you are and what you stand for, and they flesh out your commitment to the mission that inspires you and the vision that guides you. If the word "mission" describes your purpose and calling (your heart), and the word "vision" pictures where you want to be in the future (your head), then the word "values" describes the core of who you are. On an organizational level, your values dictate how you and your employees work together every day to help you fulfill your mission, follow your vision, and achieve your goals. The values by which you *actually* live—which, unfortunately, do not always mirror the values listed on a corporate website—go a long way toward determining *how* you conduct the business side of your organization, *how* you serve your customers or clients, *how* you deal with your competition, and *how* you treat the people who work for you. The organizational values that you and your people live out, much more than your mission or vision statements, tell others (both inside and outside of the organization) what you *really* believe, what you *really* cherish, and how you will act.

A quick check of current corporate websites reveals several common values shared by companies of many types. One frequently reads of values like:

- Accountability
- Balance
- Community
- Diversity
- Excellence
- Innovation
- Integrity
- Respect
- Risk taking
- Teamwork

Of course, various organizations describe such values in various ways. They don't always call them "values" or use single terms to describe them. Amazon, for example, refers to its "leadership principles," while Google uses phrases to communicate its values rather than individual words. To get an idea of what this looks like in practice, compare and contrast the following selected values listed online by two large for-profit corporations (Google and Microsoft) and by two tax-exempt ministries (Operation Blessing and World Vision).

GOOGLE: Focus on the user and all else will follow; It's best to do one thing really, really well; Fast is better than slow; You can make money without doing evil; Great just isn't good enough.

MICROSOFT: Integrity; Honesty; Openness; Personal excellence; Constructive self-criticism; Continual self-improvement; Mutual respect.

OPERATION BLESSING: Efficiency; Excellence; High Value.

WORLD VISION: We are Christian; We are committed to the poor; We value people; We are stewards; We are partners; We are responsive.

You might call values the ambassadors of an organization, the official representatives who give interested parties a clear idea of the true nature of a group. They serve as the greeters, the welcomers, the hosts, and the PR representatives of an organization. Your values tell people, both inside and outside of the organization, "This is what the organization is actually like." Your lived values determine how people perceive you.

But your stated values do more than give men and women a window into your corporate soul. They also give you guidance, strength, help, and occasional reminders. They allow others to *see* who you are, but they help you to *remain* who you are.

Your values give you guidance on how to answer tough questions.

Your values remind you to turn right when you feel an urge to turn left.

Your values help you to resolve serious conflicts. I'm especially glad for this one, because it's come in handy more than once.

Living in Line with Your Values

Years ago, I worked as the CEO of a tax-exempt, faith-based organization with a clearly defined mission and a great vision statement. We knew why we existed and where we wanted to go. We had good, strong leaders and an outstanding group of employees. Both our present and our future looked bright.

But a time came when I became aware of a serious problem, one with the potential to threaten our entire organization's culture of service.

The problem started with two of our most senior leaders, each a vice president of an important department. Both men had earned solid reputations as able leaders. Both understood the business aspects of our area of service and had recruited good people who worked hard to make our organization successful. We saw excellent growth under their leadership. To all appearances, both men seemed like ideal organizational leaders.

At some unfortunate point, however, some of the less-flattering aspects of human nature rose to the surface. These two VPs simply could not seem to work out their differences, and soon they fell into the habit of running to me with all their complaints, both about one another and about other colleagues. Shortly thereafter, of course, division appeared within our ranks.

I don't believe I've ever met a leader who enjoyed refereeing conflicts between valued employees. I know I don't. That's doubly true when the conflicts escalate into negative behavior, such as backbiting, gossip, and distrust. I prefer to believe that when I have the right people working for me at the right jobs, they can find ways to work out their professional and personal differences. I expect them to act like adults and work together for the good of the whole organization.

> *Lived-out values give substance and flesh to meaning and hope; they're concrete, real, and tangible.*

The two VPs embroiled in this unending conflict couldn't seem to grasp that their bad behavior harmed not only themselves, but everyone around them. Leaders who behave badly *always* taint the men and women who work for them and who interact regularly with them. So exactly according to script, the nasty conflict between these two leaders began to injure the whole organization. We *all* began to suffer. Communication between the two departments dropped off to almost nothing, followed closely by the evaporation of the cooperative spirit that had long characterized our organization.

Remember the old principle of one bad apple spoiling the whole bunch? Well, it certainly applied in our situation. Although I didn't consider either of these two VPs bad apples—on the contrary, I saw them both as good and talented guys who believed in our mission and who wanted the organization to succeed—their nasty behavior toward one another had to stop. Their feud had become the "bad apple," spreading rot throughout the organization.

> *A big part of your job as leader is to help your people more consistently live out your organization's stated values.*

Both leaders had forgotten, or consciously pushed to the side, our corporate values. Somehow it had slipped their minds that they worked for a faith-based organization and that they were behaving in patently unholy unprofessional ways. I have no doubt that each of these two leaders could spout all kinds of noble beliefs about honesty and working out personal differences, all with an attitude of respect. But regardless of what they *knew,* they both *did* precisely the opposite. While our corporate values insisted that we treat each other with respect and compassion, these two leaders repeatedly went behind their colleagues' backs to criticize and tear down their adversaries.

When I finally grasped the severity of the problem, I knew I had to take a firm stand for our organization's values. I'll tell you what I did a little later in this chapter. But for now, I want to refocus on what values accomplish for an organization and how they do their critical work.

Words Must Match Behavior

You never want anyone to look at how your organization does business, point to your list of corporate values, and say, "You know what? You talk the talk, but you don't walk the walk. Why should I believe anything you say?" No organization can survive long when people start calling into question its essential honesty. Without exception, the means by which you carry out your mission and vision must remain consistent with the ends.

If you want your organization to succeed, then you must train everyone you lead to provide your group's services and conduct your business in a way totally consistent with your corporate values. Your stated set of values must guide you in *everything* you do as an organization.

Can you see the utter futility of thinking that you can allow people within your organization to carry out even the noblest purposes while engaging in ignoble behaviors? People who try to live like that begin to suffer from "cognitive dissonance," a term used by psychologists to describe the inner conflict women and men feel when they claim to endorse one belief system but live out something very different. Organizations that fail to deal effectively with cognitive dissonance usually fall into such dysfunction that only sweeping, organization-wide reform can save the organization. To survive, they must reestablish consistency between the group's stated mission and vision and the behavior that group engages in to fulfill both.

People tend to be good at spotting hypocrisy—if not right away, then at least over time. When the words employed by an organization champion one set of values, but its human representatives say something very different through their unsavory actions, most observers recognize the pretense and deplore the duplicity. A damaged reputation can, with lightning speed, destroy both careers and organizations. For just a moment, let's test your memory, or at least your grasp of relatively recent history. What do the following all have in common?

- Goldman Sachs
- Gov. Mark Sanford
- Enron
- Gov. Eliot Spitzer
- Bernard Madoff
- General David Petraeus

It's really not a trick question. All of them, in one way or another, led people to believe one set of "truths," while acting on a very different set of "truths." And once their hypocrisy (and often criminal behavior) got exposed, every one of them paid a steep price. Living according to one's stated values not only honors those values but also protects one's reputation, whether in the personal or the professional realms.

If you say stealing is wrong, then you won't take a sick day and use it to go golfing.

If you say you believe in the sanctity of marriage, then you won't do anything that even hints at unfaithfulness to your spouse.

If you say you believe that "honesty is the best policy," then you will treat all your business associates fairly and with integrity.

Tax-exempt organizations and for-profit corporations alike need a set of clearly stated values that describe how their people behave. Let's say you're the leader of an organization designed to help individuals better manage their money. Suppose consumer debt counseling is one of your primary services. You've hired good people adept at analyzing a client's situation (level of debt, annual income, monthly expenditures, other financial obligations, etc.) and prescribing a plan to get the client out of debt.

> *Your job as leader is to help everyone in your organization come to grips with reality.*

Such a service-oriented organization would probably do well to adopt as a corporate value something like "financial integrity," or a similar term that describes keeping its own house in financial order. Such a stated value indicates that you strive to practice what you preach. Your *behavior* parallels your *mission* and *vision,* in other words. All three of those critical corporate pieces must remain highly congruent.

How to Foster Values-Directed Behavior

A big part of your job as leader of your organization is to help your people more consistently "walk the talk," to equip them to more effectively live out your group's stated values.

As with mission and vision, a strong sense of organizational values will never "just happen" on its own. Even if the people you work with share your passion for the corporate mission and vision, they're human, as you are. We're all imperfect human beings, each with our own peculiar selfish tendencies and personal blind spots. We mess up, get it wrong, make mistakes, and occasionally lose our moral bearings. Even the best of us sometimes act in ways that conflict with our organization's mission and values.

Smart leaders do everything they can to banish mystery from both their organizations and their own leadership styles.

But as the leader, you can make a big difference in this area by actively modeling your group's values throughout your organization. Just as you can help your people to understand, embrace, and operate out of a healthy commitment to your organizational mission and vision, so you can model and encourage all of your coworkers to behave consistently with your organizational values. That proactivity includes intentionally speaking and teaching those values, setting a good example, and offering discipline and correction when needed.

1. Consciously define, speak about, and teach your corporate values.

One of your many responsibilities as a leader is to keep yourself and the people who serve under you in line with your organization's values. But how can anyone align themselves with those values if they don't know what they are? Just as you speak constantly about your organization's mission, as you remind people continually about your organization's vision, so you must teach repeatedly about your organizational values.

And what does such teaching entail? Use your imagination. Get creative. Innovate. The best, most effective teaching occurs when your students hear *repeated* instruction in *multiple* forms and contexts, *discover* some things for themselves, and periodically get a delightful *surprise* as some unexpected insight catches them unawares. A friend of mine insists that people "get" important concepts most effectively when they are repeatedly exposed to key information on a constantly moving continuum between The Expected and The Unanticipated. When the teaching style never varies, students learn to tune out the teacher. When the teaching style looks and sounds different every time around, it tends to confuse students and focus their attention more on the style than on the substance. But a good, ever-changing mix between the two teaching poles helps people learn . . . and enjoy the learning.

2. Set a good example by living out your corporate values.
Teaching values has to start at the top. That means that the best place for you to create an organization focused on values is by making sure you both talk the talk *and* walk the walk.

Good leaders know that most people tend to follow a good example. A leader who does what she says is a leader whose employees will follow suit and apply those same values to their work.

Over the years, I've tried to be open about what I believe, about my values, and about what I think my calling is. I've also tried to be open about how my beliefs and values tend to influence how I behave and how I treat people on a day-to-day basis. I've tried to make sure that this clarity extends to my work as an organizational leader. I understand the importance of clearly communicating the values of the organizations I work for, but even more than that, I understand how vital it is that my behavior matches my words.

> *When you look for the win-win, you build beneficial working relationships, characterized by mutual respect and concern.*

3. Discipline and correct when the situation requires it.

People are people, and sometimes logic, encouragement, and clear teaching doesn't get the job done. Your job as a leader then requires you to correct and even discipline coworkers who get it wrong or who violate stated values. What does such correction and discipline look like? It may take the form of issuing stern warnings, including official reprimands in a personnel file, or other escalating consequences. And it may reach the point where a parting of the ways becomes the only feasible solution.

No good leader enjoys making such drastic decisions, but that's when you learn the truth of the axiom, "It's lonely at the top." As the one charged with the all-important task of standing guard over your organization's mission, vision, and values, you must recognize that times will come when you have to say to yourself, "The mission is bigger than any individual."

Most conflicts end well when you appeal to your organization's values and then back up those values with a stiff personal resolve. But not all conflicts end on such an upbeat note. I can tell you from personal experience that sometimes, after trying everything possible to solve a problem, I've had no choice but to say, "I'm sorry, but we have decided to go in a different direction."

It may help to realize that even the termination of someone's employment can reflect and support an organization's values. There is such a thing as addition by subtraction. Poison is generally incompatible with health. It never feels good to fire someone, but again: The mission is bigger than any individual.[9]

Strive for Balance

Creating a work atmosphere with a strong focus on your organization's values will require you to strike a balance between high expectations and genuine concern for your employees. Every person who works for you is uniquely made, and each person has individual strengths, weaknesses, fears, and insecurities.

Compassion is one of Adventist Health System's most important values. We apply that value to our patients and their families by treating them with kindness and empathy, and we also strive to apply that value to the individuals who work for and with us, including those who need extra help in understanding and applying our values. This doesn't mean we lower our high standards, that we enable behavior that opposes our values, or that we fail to hold people accountable for their behavior. It simply means that we see every person who works for us as an imperfect human being who has the ability to grow and become great at what he or she does. And we maintain that perspective while upholding our corporate values.

It isn't easy to equip the people who work for you to live out your organization's stated values. It's hard work that starts with you clearly communicating your expectations and requirements, and then living up to them yourself. You'll need to take on the role of teacher and disciplinarian, and you'll need to play that role with an eye toward your people's personal flaws.

It's sometimes difficult, always exciting work—but it's the kind of work that will help make your organization world class in every way.

Time for Action

Let's suppose you've done everything in your power to communicate and instill your organization's values in the people who work for you. You've spoken the right words and set the right example, and it seems that most everyone has embraced your instruction.

But, human nature being what it is, you find that a few people in your organization still don't quite "get it." Maybe they're just stragglers who take longer to catch on to something new, or maybe they *completely* get it but have certain "blind spots" that cause some kind of disparity between their behavior and the values you espouse. Such situations will put to the test all of your skills as a leader and a communicator. How should you respond to them? Let me suggest an answer by returning to the story of the two "rival" vice presidents who worked for me years ago.

After working with these men for some time and encouraging them to turn the corner and bury the proverbial hatchet, still the situation did not improve. I finally came to the place where I simply could no longer accept the behavior of these two leaders, especially since it directly contradicted several of our organization's stated values. I knew that if I, as the CEO, didn't deal decisively with their destructive behavior, it would spread like a deadly cancer.

At the same time, I considered both men quality colleagues whom I really didn't want to lose. I decided that if I had to take some extra time to instruct, correct, and admonish them—or something even more severe—I would consider it time well spent. I wanted to see them rehabilitated.

I called both men into my office.

"Look, you're not kids anymore," I said. "You're in senior levels of responsibility, and you should be leading in a way that models our values. People look to you to model professional behavior, but what you've been doing is unprofessional."

I let my words sink in for a moment, and then I appealed to our corporate values as a faith-based organization. After a few minutes of stern lecture, complete with grim CEO face, I thought we'd solved the problem.

Unfortunately, we hadn't.

When the same cantankerous behavior continued, I tried hiking the communication up a notch. I met with each man privately to discuss how his behavior was hurting our organization. I let them both know that they were damaging our reputation and our ability to live out our mission. I implored them to act like leaders. Problem solved, right?

Again, no.

Over the next several weeks, it became apparent that these two VPs hadn't taken *any* steps to change their dysfunctional ways. If anything, their behavior grew worse. The time had come for a final appeal—an ultimatum.

I can be extremely blunt when the situation calls for it, and though I didn't want to lose either of these two talented, dedicated men, I let them know in plain language that I could not accept their behavior and that it was going to stop.

"Gentlemen, what you two have been doing cannot be tolerated within this organization," I declared. "This has consumed all kinds of time and energy, which I can't afford. I do not have time to referee your fights. That is not my purpose here.

Most people won't reach the heart level expressed by a corporate mission until they experience the organization's values every day, primarily in little ways.

"The bottom line is that the two of you are going to have to learn to work together. You *are* going to stop coming to me with personal complaints about each other and you *will* work out your differences together. And if you don't, I'm going to terminate both of you."

The room got very quiet. They both sheepishly left my office.

And then they got busy working out their differences.

Someone once said rightly that necessity is the mother of invention. It took the real threat of being fired to get these two men to find a way to work together for the common good. It took a grave warning of their mutual, imminent dismissal to prompt them to learn how to communicate as adults.

Even while I threatened them with joblessness, however, I wanted both of these leaders to become great at what they did. I wanted my team to flourish. I knew these men had a lot to offer our organization. They both knew that I valued them and liked them personally . . . but even so, they both knew I was dead serious about the consequences, should they fail to find a way to work together.

Within a short period of time, the deplorable behavior that had threatened our organization completely stopped. These two leaders went far beyond simply learning to coexist in a tough work environment, and over time, grew to truly respect, and, I believe, even care about one another. As they spent time talking and proactively working out their personal and professional differences, they became not merely good colleagues, but good friends.

And, by the way, their departments began working together better than they ever had.

Will this positive outcome happen in every case? Probably not. But as keepers of your organization's values, your leaders and staff need to know that they will be held responsible for practicing those values.

Behavior must match words. That is the only way your stated values will make a real difference inside and outside of your organization.

8

The Hazards Ahead

How Values Serve as Guardrails to Protect from Serious Mishaps

On a pleasant fall night when spectacular autumn foliage attracted the usual seasonal visitors to New England, a tour bus from Kansas City, Missouri, whisked forty happy passengers along the scenic Kancamagus Highway. About ten miles outside of Conway, New Hampshire, a car heading in the opposite direction suddenly veered out of its lane, crossed the center line, and struck the bus. The car almost instantly erupted into flames, killing its two passengers.

The bus driver did all he could to avoid the crash, but the force of the impact pushed his vehicle off the road, sending it hurtling toward a steep embankment and a river far below. How many fatalities would the accident claim?

Only two, it turned out. No one on the bus died, although sixteen of its elderly passengers received minor medical treatment. Fortunately, the bus didn't tumble into the cold river. It didn't even plunge over the embankment. Why not?

Guardrails.

When the bus struck some guardrails strategically placed along the edge of the embankment, the vehicle ground to a halt without toppling over. Without those guardrails, according to one New Hampshire State trooper, "They would have gone down the ravine for sure." [10]

All over the nation, states are busily at work installing various kinds of guardrails along medians, dangerous curves, bridges, and other spots of treacherous road where vehicles have a tendency to veer off into trouble. States from North Carolina to Missouri, Michigan to Washington, have made large investments in guardrails while citing studies that show such safety systems can almost immediately result in a reduction of fatal crashes by up to 100 percent and a decrease in vehicle-on-vehicle crashes by up to 60 percent. [11]

Guardrails work, essentially by helping to keep vehicles where they're supposed to be. When someone goes to sleep at the wheel of an errant car, truck, or bus and starts heading for a cliff, strong and well-placed guardrails can keep the driver's vehicle from plummeting into the abyss.

I started thinking about guardrails when I visited a website that lists just short of a hundred core values adopted by companies from a wide assortment of industries. The Cirion Group, which compiled the list, titles its collection, "The non-negotiable guardrails guiding your decisions."[12] Just as there are many kinds of roadside guardrails to protect travelers in a variety of environments, so are there many kinds of core values that protect organizations on their unique corporate journeys.

Think of your *mission* as your ultimate destination, the endpoint reason why you're on this trip at all. Your *vision* is your planned route to get you to your destination, a set of plans (which could change, depending on fluctuating conditions) designed to help you navigate from where you are to where you want to be. In this extended metaphor, your *values* function to keep you safely on the road and moving toward your journey's planned end. Should you fall asleep at the wheel or get distracted, your values serve as life-saving guardrails to prevent you from driving your company car off a cliff.

Just as differing road conditions call for an assortment of guardrails appropriate to each environment, so differing organizations and industries call for various kinds of values, each suitable for their own environments. The values that suit one organization extremely well may not apply to another group at all.

In this chapter, I'd like to unpack just one or two of the values that shape and guard our culture within Adventist Health System. I do so, not to suggest that we have made superior choices or to encourage you to adopt what works for us, but rather to flesh out a bit of how values actually work within an organization. And since I know our organization better than I know anyone else's, I'll use some of our values as examples.

The Values We Live By

Several years ago, we developed a list of core values and an acronym that would help us to remember them. When you take the first letter of each of these values, we get the acronym ICBEST, which stands for:

Integrity – When one's words or actions create trust
Compassion – Meeting individual needs with kindness
Balance – Harmony in one's mind, body, and spirit
Excellence – Providing extraordinary care and service
Stewardship – Responsibly managing resources
Teamwork – Valuing others' diversity and perspective

Elsewhere in this book you've seen how the values of balance and stewardship play out in the way we function every day. In this chapter, I'd like to focus primarily on the first value listed, integrity. I do that not only because it's first on the list, but also because I believe everyone, and most especially leaders, should strive to become persons of integrity.

A number of authors and speakers have been credited with the saying, "Integrity is doing the right thing, even when no one is watching." While I love that definition, I would add that integrity also means doing what you know is right regardless of the personal cost.

Both individuals and organizations should care deeply about integrity, because a good name is an asset of inestimable worth. The way you and others in your organization do things impacts your reputation and will either earn or lose your customers' trust and confidence.

Customers, clients, vendors, and curious observers all watch closely to see whether individuals and organizations really live out their mission and core values. When you consistently demonstrate the integrity it takes to do this well, you inspire trust and confidence in your brand.

The Currency of Trust

When you think of the word "trust," what comes to mind? Usually it's a personal relationship, such as a marriage or a close friendship. When you trust someone in such a relationship, you put your confidence in the individual. You expect the person to keep his or her promises, to remain faithful, to stand by you, to give you reliable support, and to tell you the truth. You depend on the person to act with integrity.

While your business relationships differ in many ways from your closest personal relationships, the principle of trust applies in both contexts. Just as building a happy marriage means establishing and keeping your spouse's trust, so too establishing strong leadership in your organization means earning the trust of the people who work with and for you.

Can the people in your organization rely on you and your work? Do they have to frequently second-guess your decisions or wonder whether you have their best interests at heart?

I've spent many years of my professional life managing CEOs. I make it a point to tell these leaders, over and over again, "Trust is the coin of the realm."

In many ways, trust is like money. You can spend it, you can bank it, or you can invest it. And if you're not careful, through foolish choices you can totally drain your account of it. Leaders can do this by failing to uphold their mission and values, through poor communication, by fudging on the truth, or by neglecting to demonstrate integrity in how they deal with people.

Good leaders understand the importance of making regular deposits in the bank of trust. Every time you keep your word, fulfill a promise, stand up for a colleague, tell a hard truth with compassion, or otherwise show yourself to be a person of integrity, you make a trust deposit. You don't get an account at this bank just because you're a leader. You open it and make deposits to it whenever your people see you leading with integrity or living according to the principles you espouse.

> *Transparency builds trust in those who work with you and for you.*

Do you want to know something alarming about this bank of trust? While I've seen many examples over the years of effective leaders who made regular deposits, I can't think of a single time when a leader emptied his or her account and then managed to build it up again. When people lose trust in their leader, it's pretty much over. Account balances in the bank of trust that drop to zero or get overdrawn make it extremely difficult, and perhaps impossible, for a leader to regain those lost funds. They almost always have to switch banks and try to start over somewhere else.

TELLING THE (HARD) TRUTH INCREASES DEPOSITS IN THE TRUST BANK

I believe one of the most important values you can possess as a leader is telling the truth—even when it is difficult to do so. Honesty is imperative as both a personal value and an organizational value.

Telling the truth, of course, can sometimes pose a real challenge. Your people may ask you some direct, difficult questions. Suppose you have to make some organizational changes. What do you say when worried employees ask you about pay raises or cuts, promotions or demotions, or if they can count on having a job in a month because they're expecting their first baby? I can tell you from personal experience that it's a struggle to be honest with people in such situations. But I can also tell you that, if you agree to answer the question and don't say something like, "I'll have to get back to you on that," it's always better to give a truthful response. You don't have to spill every last detail, of course, but if you give an answer, make it an honest one.

> *Ambivalent answers and wobbly directions always erode trust and create vastly more stress for everyone.*

Many leaders feel the temptation to change their tune,

depending on the audience. They may say one thing to a colleague, another to a small group, a third thing in a town hall-type meeting, and sometimes still another when addressing the whole organization. That never ends well. You can make regular deposits to the bank of trust only when you speak the truth in every context. Reality is reality, and your job as a leader is to help everyone in your organization come to grips with it.

When you lead a large and complex organization with a big staff featuring a wide range of specialties, mindsets, and assumptions, it's easy to drift into an audience-pleasing mode. Your efforts to connect with specific people may tempt you to "reshape reality" according to what you think they want to hear. But a drift like that leads you only into a snowbank, not the bank of trust.

Do your best to speak the truth, period. Don't water down essential deposits in the bank of trust. If you can't speak the truth, then keep silent. Quiet honesty is better than loud falsehood.

Building Trust Requires Dependability and Consistency

Employees naturally want to feel that they can depend on their leaders. They want to believe that those in positions of authority are consistent men or women of integrity and that they truly care about their subordinates.

Do your people believe they can depend on you? Or do they have little idea what you may do from one day to the next?

Building trust has little bearing on whether you're the warm and fuzzy type or the no-nonsense, bottom-line type. I know leaders of both kinds who succeed, and leaders of both kinds who struggle. Your personality type has little to do with it.

Years ago, two executives I'll call Jennifer and Melissa worked for me at a hospital. While both were outstanding leaders, their personalities couldn't have been more different. Jennifer had an incredibly warm, sociable personality, and just about everyone loved being around her. People sought her out, simply because she had a natural way of making them feel liked and important. Melissa, on the other hand, was a classic introvert. While she went out of her way to respect those around her, people often perceived her as a little tough and hard.

Organizations that lack a well-defined list of values, or that fail to make them a key part of their culture, are destined for mediocrity.

Despite their personality differences, however, Jennifer and Melissa worked together successfully over a long period of time. I trusted Jennifer every bit as much as I trusted Melissa, and I found that both inspired a great deal of trust in those who worked under them.

How do you suppose these two leaders, so opposite in personality and style, could make equally impressive deposits in the bank of trust? Their people saw each of them as dependable and consistent, because they consistently made their decisions based on the same corporate values.

Most people don't mind working for a demanding leader, so long as that leader clearly and consistently communicates what she expects and so long as she lives and works according to the values she espouses. Most employees tend to *thrive* under that kind of leader.

You build deposits in the bank of trust by being a dependable, consistent leader who holds dear the value of integrity.

How Transparency Builds Trust

Over the past several years, we have seen several disastrous examples of what can happen when business professionals fail to disclose their riskiest and most questionable business practices. When those practices finally came to light, untold numbers of victims found themselves suddenly broke. Many of those unscrupulous leaders wound up in prison.

We make it a point in our organization to go out of our way to ensure that no one surpasses us in terms of full disclosure. We do this, not to avoid getting in trouble with the authorities, but because it's one of our values as an organization. We think it's the right thing to do. We want to do whatever we can to ensure that we are 100 percent transparent about our business practices and that we hide nothing from view.

You can read a transparent person like a book. When she speaks her mind, you know she's being honest. She's a straight shooter who has no hidden agendas, nothing to hide, and clearly defines and explains her guiding principles.

Smart leaders do everything they can to banish mystery, both from their organizations and from their own leadership style. Having an air of mystery may work well for a movie character whose true identity doesn't come to light until just before the final credits roll, but "mysterious" leaders too often lead their organizations into decline.

Don't leave people guessing about your principles and motives. Make sure they know your guiding principles and convictions, what you expect of them, and what you hope to accomplish. Transparency builds trust in those who work with you and for you.

Trusted Companies and Leaders Learn How to Communicate Clearly

I've seen the scenario played out more times than I care to remember. Two people with conflicting ideas about some project meet with their leader to straighten things out. After an hour or two, they walk out of the same meeting, in the same office, with the same leader, both believing they have a firm grasp of their instructions. But when they compare notes, they find they left the same meeting with totally opposite impressions.

How can that happen? How can one question appear to generate two answers? How can a meeting held to clarify a situation result in even more confusion? In almost every case, it happens because the leader has not clearly communicated his or her decision. In a mistaken attempt to mollify the "loser," the decision comes out garbled and indistinct—creating losers all around.

None of us like to upset our colleagues, so we can feel tempted to offer muddled, wishy-washy communication, to hedge on the facts, and to give vague explanations. But ambivalent answers and wobbly directions, though they may temporarily head off heated confrontation, always erode trust and create vastly more stress for everyone.

Well-functioning families nearly always exhibit clear, concise communication, whether between adults, between adults and children, and even between children. Children, especially, need a clear, unambiguous "yes" or an equally clear, unambiguous "no." Without such clear communication, confusion and frustration and hurt feelings almost always result. A home environment characterized by clear, unambiguous communication naturally leads to a happier, more secure environment in which everyone in the home can grow and thrive.

The same principle gets played out every day in our hospitals and clinics. Our hospital directors and members of their medical staffs occasionally have disputes over things like which specialties and practices they should pursue, which physicians have the appropriate credentials and backgrounds to perform certain procedures, and how specific processes should be handled. In situations like these, our leaders must prepare themselves to give highly principled and clearly stated answers. They must take into account our mission, our values, the likely financial implications of a particular decision, and the skills and abilities of the people who work for them. They must take care to make every decision with an eye toward what seems best for the facility and for Adventist Health System as a whole.

We encourage and train our leaders to give highly principled and clear answers to the tough questions they have to field. Expedient, temporary answers won't do, nor will ambivalence or equivocating.

Of course, "clear and unequivocal" does not mean "rude and abrupt." While I rarely struggle with being extremely direct when the situation calls for it, I also recognize that I never have a reason to speak insensitively to anyone or to belittle their concerns or ideas. I have learned that clear communication—even when I have to give a "no" to some specific request—can go much more smoothly when I respond with empathy and when I acknowledge another person's interests as legitimate.

> *Think of your corporate values as life-saving guardrails that prevent you from driving your company car off a cliff.*

When you explain a decision, even one based on your organization's clearly stated principles, be prepared to hear that someone won't like what you have to say. But honesty and straightforwardness, flavored with gentleness and empathy, never has to destroy a good working relationship. Learn to use them instead to help build a stronger, healthier work environment.

At the end of the day, remember this: When your decisions and actions rest on your organization's mission and values, and not merely on your own personal interests, your people will find it much easier to rise above their own personal interests in order to accept a decision that doesn't go quite their way.

Over and over I've seen how clear communication from a leader who has integrity fosters trust in his or her organization.

Insist on Mutual Respect

Shortly after I started leading one of the hospitals in our system, a supporter of the institution who would later become a board member invited me to his office. He told me he had scheduled a dinner with a group of physicians and wondered if I would attend, to make it something of a get-to-know-the-new-leader affair.

I had become aware that many of these physicians felt irritated about the physician-hospital organization (PHO) through which we provided insurance to our employees. These private physicians didn't feel that the PHO paid them a sufficient wage. They felt unsettled about that and unhappy about a number of other issues.

That evening we had a nice dinner and pleasant table interaction. But then I decided to pop the question: "Do you have any issues that especially concern you?"

One man, a physician with a bombastic reputation, started in. He didn't address the central issues but began hammering at the executive in charge of our PHO. It got personal and quite abusive.

I admit, that's a hot button for me. As a leader, you have to be pretty thick-skinned when someone criticizes you personally, but it's a different matter entirely when someone attacks an associate. You cannot allow character assassination.

So I shot back. I made it clear that I could not tolerate anyone maligning our people in this manner. "If this meeting is about attacking someone's character and personal integrity, then I will have to leave," I said.

After I laid down that boundary, the meeting became quite pleasant again. The interaction mellowed and we got down to discussing important issues.

Later, the man who'd burst out with his attack apologized to the host. He confessed that he hadn't sensed what he was doing. The host replied that no leader worth his salt would allow one of their own to get slammed in that way in front of a group.

And that is precisely the issue. Public humiliation is out of bounds, always. No matter how bad things seem to be going, a good leader never allows an associate to get savaged for whatever current troubles are roiling the waters.

One of my values insists that the relationship between a leader and his colleagues must have an element of mutual respect, or trust will be lost.

Trust, Respect, and Power Struggles

When both parties in a business relationship approach each other with respect and expect to receive something of value from the relationship, then finding a "win-win solution" is possible. But the moment the dialogue turns to monologue, or becomes a personal attack, or switches to an ultimatum, then that relationship has been compromised. It's no longer about finding a win-win solution but about taking control. It's devolved into coercive power and dehumanizing force.

The word "values" describes your organizational soul.

If individuals or groups believe they can dictate terms and issue unconditional demands, then a leader might as well give away the keys to the place. You cannot work effectively with your associates unless they respect you, and they won't respect you unless they know you will stand up for your organization's values and goals.

The problem gets no better from the other side of the room. Some leaders love to lord it over their people. They make unconditional demands. They give ultimatums. That doesn't work, either. For it tends to break down trust rather than build it.

While servant-leaders must be willing to confront and draw necessary boundaries, they must never forget the principle of win-win. Do you want something out of a relationship? Then you need to bring something into that relationship. The minute it becomes one-sided—the minute one party's doing all the taking and one party's doing all the giving—then it's no longer a healthy working relationship.

Do everything you can to ensure that you build mutually beneficial working relationships, characterized by mutual respect and concern. Don't focus on your position but instead on fostering a healthy relationship with your employees. Always look for the win-win.

In order to accomplish that, you'll have to work hard at building the bank of trust. A leader with integrity—one who is frank and honest about his principles and steady and consistent in his actions—can build that bank by creating healthy win-win relationships and not giving in to one-sided power struggles.

It Really Does Work

Remember the illustration that opened this chapter about the value of guardrails? Not long ago I came across another headline from the great state of Michigan that announced, "Median Cable Guardrail System Helps Save 10 Lives in I-94 Crash."[13] The accompanying article described how a three-year safety initiative by the Michigan Department of Transportation paid "big dividends" when the driver of a van from Minnesota carrying ten people lost control outside of Coloma and struck a section of the newly installed cable guardrail. Although the van rolled "several times," it never crossed the median into opposing traffic.

"Our new system did exactly what it was designed to do," said State Transportation Director Kirk T. Steudle. "By preventing the vehicle from crossing over the median, our cable guardrail system is proving its worth. While 10 people were hurt in the crash, there were no fatalities and the lives of innocent people on both sides of the roadway were protected."

While your corporate values may not be able, by themselves, to keep your organization from serious mishaps, you can ensure that you stay on the road toward your ultimate destination by installing, securing, and maintaining strong values. When major conflicts or personal collisions occur—and they will—having strong values in place will function like effective guardrails. You may need repairs, but you won't go flying off of a cliff into a deep ravine.

> *A leader who does as he or she says is a leader whose employees will follow suit and apply those same values to their work.*

I don't know what kind of values your organization needs. I don't know the contours of your terrain or the nature of your environment. I can't tell you where your sharp curves might hide or where people tend to fall asleep at the wheel and veer into oncoming traffic.

But I don't need to know any of that, because I don't lead your organization. You, on the other hand, need to know all of it. If you're not sure where your organization needs some strong guardrails/values in place, then do whatever you have to in order to find out. If you can see some potentially hazardous spots ahead, then put up some appropriate guardrails/values. When you do so, then regardless of the mishaps ahead, you'll also be able to say, "Our system did exactly what it was designed to do."

9

Moving from the Head to the Heart

How Good Values Help You Win Regardless of Uncertainty

EVERY HUMAN BEING ON THE PLANET HAS A critical need for two transcendent things. None of us can find real happiness without either one.

Each of us needs both *meaning* and *hope.*

Not everyone recognizes they have such a need, of course. Maybe you've worked with someone who, at least on the surface, didn't appear to have the slightest interest in either meaning or hope. He or she goes about a daily life of driving to work, eating lunch, listening to the radio, and buying groceries, without once wondering, *Is this all there is to life?* or what Dante meant when, in his classic, *The Inferno,* he envisioned this sign at the Gates of Hell, "Abandon all hope, ye who enter here."

Human beings can function without conscious reference to meaning and hope so long as they have full stomachs and healthy bank accounts. But take away those things, or bring in some terrible threat to life itself, and *all* of us start pondering the meaning of our lives and whether any hope yet remains for us. And often, our minds begin traveling down that road because of what happens at work.

What answers do the people who work for us find when they arrive Monday morning for another workweek? Do they walk into a culture that gives them hope and points to meaning, or do they feel worse at the end of the workday than at the beginning? I believe with all my heart that it is our duty as leaders to help build within our organizations a culture full of both meaning and hope. And the values we nurture in the workplace play a critical role in the development of both.

From Head to Heart

To feel truly happy, human beings need to believe that their lives truly count for something and that their future really does look bright. They need meaning and a sense of purpose, as well as hope, the justifiable expectation that many good things lie ahead for them.

While it may be too much to imagine that a mere job could provide them with both meaning and hope, it should not be too much to expect that their work could at least get them moving in that direction. After all, two of the key elements of organizational success—mission and vision—focus directly on both meaning and hope.

A strong mission provides an organization with a

lasting purpose, a profound reason for being, something big and worthwhile to work for that makes it a pleasure to get up each morning. Mission, in other words, gives us a deep sense of meaning in our work.

A compelling vision provides an organization with a captivating destination to reach, an attractive target to shoot for, an important goal to accomplish that will help the organization to fulfill its mission in a particular time and place. Vision, in other words, gives us a potent sense of hope that we can achieve something of great significance.

Both mission and vision, however, are primarily cognitive. They express what we *think* about our purpose and where we *think* we need to go in order to achieve our purpose. Both are crucial and both are wonderful, but in order to enjoy a life-sustaining conviction that our lives have deep meaning and that we're headed someplace terrific, we need more than inspiring thoughts.

And that's precisely where values enter the picture.

Lived-out values give substance and flesh to meaning and hope. They're concrete, real, and tangible. You can see them in the smiles of coworkers, hear them in a story celebrating an associate who chose to go the extra mile. In short, an organization's values—when lived out and regularly practiced—create a healthy, positive, life-affirming culture. Values connect the head with the heart and so make visible the otherwise invisible.

Mission + Vision + Values = Culture

An organization's culture grows out of its unique mixture of mission, vision, and values. All three key elements work together to create whatever culture you have. In the same way, it takes all three elements to reach the heart.

You might say that mission builds a highway between the head and the heart, vision supplies the trucks that use the highway, and values put the gas in the trucks' tanks that enable them to rumble up and down the highway to deliver their precious cargo. A problem with any of these three key elements grounds your whole fleet.

I consider mission, and meaning in life, to be so important that I used to make it a point to speak to all new employees about it. Nobody grows and develops as a well-rounded human being without paying attention to their life's meaning. I used to tell our newcomers, "If you don't think you can find real meaning in life here, then I urge you to keep looking until you find it *someplace*." I got a lot of strange looks, but I meant it. Back then, and still today, I want all of our employees to take pride in what we do. I want them to experience a culture of both hope and meaning.

What Is Culture?

If you claim to embrace a certain set of values—let's say, integrity, compassion, balance, excellence, stewardship, and trust—and outsiders can walk into your organization on any given day and find the people there behaving according to those values, then you have a healthy culture. If you have skewed values, however, or if your people don't tend to live out your stated values, then you have an unhealthy culture. And to be honest, it usually doesn't take people long to figure it out. I can usually sense the general health of an organizational culture in a short visit.

Your mission, vision, and values must be highly congruent. They all have to point in the same direction. If the average person on the street senses dissonance between your mission and your values, then you're in big-time trouble. Again, it's usually not hard to gauge the health of an organization's culture. You see it everywhere in behaviors, actions, and words. You sense it when you walk around and listen to people talk. If you say, for example, that your mission is to extend the healing ministry of Christ (the Adventist Health System mission) and your values are rooted in ICBEST, but a visitor to your organization sees indicators of a lack of integrity, then the culture is inconsistent with the mission and there is an enormous problem.

People "get" important concepts most effectively when they are repeatedly exposed to key information on a constantly moving continuum between The Expected and The Unanticipated.

Let's extend the illustration a bit. Suppose a visitor hangs around your organization for a whole month, going everywhere and talking to a large percentage of your employees . . . but never once sees anyone acting with compassion. That would be a problem, wouldn't it? I immediately think of the Scripture that describes how Jesus saw a large crowd and "had compassion on them and healed their sick" (Matthew 14:14, NIV). The Scriptures make it clear that Christ exhibited compassion, particularly when he was healing. So if we claim to extend the healing ministry of Christ and yet don't habitually display compassion, then something has gone wrong somewhere.

Good leaders continually watch for any incongruity between their mission, their vision, and their values. All three have to line up so that observers will say, "Yes, your stated values really do complement your mission. How you behave lines up with your avowed purpose. Your organization has a great culture."

People should always be able to look at your organization and make such an observation, because your values shouldn't change any more than your mission does. They both stay constant. Vision can and should change because of fluctuating circumstances, but not mission and values, the two anchors of every successful organization. Anytime those two conflict with one another, you are heading for trouble.

A Difference between Mission and Values

Although your mission should be big, your values often will express themselves in little things. They're not about grand speeches. They're about small, common, everyday actions that characterize both you and your people. You know you're creating a healthy culture when your big mission gets articulated thousands of times every day, throughout your organization, in little but meaningful practical displays of your values.

People watch the decisions you make and wonder: *Do they really line up with your published values?* Every day, they interpret the little things that happen. They can't help but do it. They want to work in a place that consistently lives out its stated values.

Frontline managers play a critical role here, because those are the leaders your employees see every day. If you oversee a large organization, most of your coworkers may not get a glimpse of you for weeks or even months on end. *You* may live out your corporate values, but if your frontline managers don't, then you have a major problem. Building a healthy culture requires that the vast majority of the people in your organization, starting with you and your leaders, live out your core values. And usually that "living out" involves doing small things repeatedly, day in and day out.

Use Values to Move toward Mission

I believe that mission provides the bulk of what motivates people to get enthused about their jobs, day after day. In most cases, however, you can't immediately reach a person at that core, heart level. It takes something else to move them from the head to the heart.

New hires may well say to you, “I’m so excited about working for an organization that has this mission and purpose.” Usually they mean it. But then, after about ninety days, they crawl out of bed one morning feeling a little tired, and maybe the day before didn’t go well. Perhaps they encountered people within the organization whose behavior didn’t match what they rightly expected to see. What happens then? Their failure to experience the group’s stated values will erode whatever intellectual connection to the mission they had initially.

But if they get up one day feeling tired and a little cranky, go to work, and find their department coworkers living out those values, their manager passionately practicing them, and even unfamiliar employees incarnating the same values, then that experience will carry them through the tough times. The mission that initially so appealed to their heads now carves out a permanent place in their hearts. And so they morph from individuals who need reminders of the mission to persons who enthusiastically promote the mission.

Even the termination of someone’s employment can reflect and support an organization’s values.

What makes the difference? Not big speeches about the mission, but consistent expressions of the values. Most people won’t reach that heart level until they experience your values every day, primarily in little ways.

A Healthy Culture Transfers Its Values

Suppose you hire a young person who joins you early in her career, an individual who has not yet learned the principle of personal accountability. But as a result of working daily with world-class managers who consistently display personal accountability, that young woman begins learning what it means to be personally accountable.

This newly acquired value starts to benefit her not only in her work life, but in her personal life and home life. She becomes a better citizen. She becomes more reliable, more dependable. She makes better decisions about the challenges she must face. As the values consistently expressed around her start becoming her own values, your organization finds it easier and easier to fulfill its mission.

This is why it's well worth your while as the leader to do everything you can to instill your corporate values in your managers. Do whatever you can, not only to help them understand the values, but to consistently practice them, day in and day out. Managers who live out your values have an almost incalculable effect on your organization. You might say they have golden hands.

Have you ever seen the advertisement in which some guy says, "I've never shaken a gold hand before"? The commercial promotes some TV device that lets people easily record the shows they want. The man in the ad says, "The guy who invented *that* must have hands made of gold." Your managers who live out your organization's values also have hands of gold.

Best of all, their Midas touch is transferable. Make sure they know what a huge role they play in your organization's success.

Different Beliefs, Same Values

I'd like to share an interesting statistic with you about our organization and how it relates to our values. Years ago, we ran some numbers about the percentage of Adventists who worked for Florida Hospital. The figure came in at just under 17 percent. That meant that more than 83 percent of our employees identified themselves as something other than Adventists. And yet, as a group, they consistently embodied our values and championed our mission.

Do you find that statistic as interesting as I do?

It tells me that the vast majority of people in an organization may have beliefs different from those held by the founders or top management of the organization, and yet the organization can thrive. It demonstrates that if your values are right and consistent with your mission, and the people within your organization consistently live out those values most of the time, then by definition you have a healthy culture.

No group can become world class without a strong sense of values.

You don't pick your values out of a hat. You don't choose them simply because they look good in a newspaper article or spruce up a website. Your values have to reflect your mission; and when you train your people to live out those values, and they do so consistently, then you set yourself up for success, regardless of the personal beliefs or backgrounds of your employees.

Of course, you'll get all kinds of employees. Some of them will make your job easy, some will make it difficult, and the vast majority will need your help to live out the consistently expressed values that produce a healthy culture.

Three Types of Employees

My experience tells me that employees tend to come in three basic varieties: Hard Chargers, Scoundrels, and the Broad Middle. If you were to plot them on a graph, you'd get a classic bell-shaped curve.

1. Hard Chargers

Perhaps the top 10 percent of the people you work with will be Hard Chargers. You don't have to do a single thing to motivate them; they are totally self-motivated. They go from zero to sixty in about two seconds, so just get out of their way. These are dynamic people.

2. Scoundrels

Another 2 to 5 percent of the individuals you hire will reveal themselves as Scoundrels. There's not a thing in the world you can do on the face of this earth to motivate them, and the sooner you get them out of your organization, the better.

When I taught college chemistry, I used to get several

panicky freshman nursing students who took the course only because they had to. To set their minds at ease, I used to walk in on the first day and say, "Nothing would make me happier than to have every one of you pass this course. I'm going to do my level best to get all of you to the place where you can pass. I'm not going to dilute it; I'm not going to lower the bar just so you can pass. If I did that, I would be doing you a disservice. But if you're willing to work hard, please don't worry." For those who needed extra help, I held optional sessions outside of normal class time. The result? Over many years of teaching, I had at least a 95 percent pass rate. Almost never did a hard-working student find it impossible to earn a passing grade.

But I also had a few students—almost invariably intelligent and bright kids with all kinds of mental horsepower—who goofed off. I used to tell *them*, "I will lose absolutely no sleep whatsoever about you flunking this course. As matter of fact, if you are very, very bright and you don't care, I will flunk you with pleasure."

In all my years outside of academia, I've rarely had a problem with employees except for the small percentage of Scoundrels who just didn't care. And there's nothing you can do with them except to get them to move on.

3. The Broad Middle

In all likelihood, more than 85 percent of the people you hire will fit into the Broad Middle. These people want to work hard. They want to conduct themselves responsibly, be diligent, and do a good job for you.

You can help them achieve their desires by insisting on high levels of performance. Make it clear that you expect them to live out your corporate values so that all of you, together, can fulfill your corporate mission. Do not accept substandard performance, and don't allow anyone to make excuses for sloppy or lazy work.

I've mentioned before that in tax-exempt cultures in general (and faith-based cultures in particular), we have a tendency to shrink back from insisting on top performance. While we always want to treat people with respect and dignity, however, we can never let anyone tell us that it's somehow wrong to demand high performance—and the right word is "demand." Demand it of yourself, and demand it of your people.

The funny thing is that when you agree to lead a sloppy and loose organization where no one has ever demanded performance, and you make it abundantly clear that a new day has come and that sloppiness and laziness will no longer be tolerated, the vast majority will blossom, like flowers. They will get excited because they *want* to do well and they *want* to succeed, if only someone will lead them boldly and show them what to do.

A leader must actively model the organization's values.

Some will feel threatened because they have not performed well, but poor performance usually comes from one of three sources: (1) lack of adequate training; (2) working at the wrong job; (3) a bad attitude. You and your leadership team can correct the first two problems. For the third one, see "Scoundrels" above. Frankly, you can't do much about a bad attitude, so get those people out of your organization as quickly as possible. Your Hard Chargers have had to put up with them for too long already, and if you delay in getting rid of the bad attitudes, you may lose your top performers. So lose the Scoundrels and watch what happens. Both the Broad Middle and your Hard Chargers will soar.

Culture Forms Slowly

Imagine that you've been hired as the leader of an underperforming organization with a fine mission. You decide that you need to emphasize the value of integrity. So you call your leaders together one day and you tell them, "From now on, we will make integrity the cornerstone value of this organization."

You're done, right? It's over. They've all "got it." Henceforth, integrity will characterize everything in your organization. You've announced it and you've insisted on it. Done.

Oh, if only it worked that way.

While a culture can become diseased in almost no time at all, it takes a *very* long time to build a strong, healthy one. Human beings are not easily convinced. It usually takes many months and even years to form the kind of culture you want.

Once it gets deeply embedded in an organization,

however, it becomes extremely powerful—perhaps the most potent tool you have. Someone once said, "Culture trumps strategy every day of the week." You need both tools, of course, but the best strategy or vision statement in the world will do you little good if you try to implement it within a sick culture.

Building a healthy culture takes time. It almost always takes longer than you think it should. But when you keep at it, teaching and encouraging and equipping your people to live out the organization's values, you set yourself up for a much longer period of success.

Telling Stories Reinforces Your Values

One of the hospitals I led had long hosted what it calls a "Leadership Weekend." This is a time, usually once a year during the fall, when all the top leaders of the organization go away for a retreat weekend to review strategic plans, discuss future initiatives, and reconnect around the company mission. Shortly after I arrived, I started using Friday evening to tell success stories, real-world tales of what we had done for patients.

> *Since public humiliation is always out of bounds, a good leader never allows an associate to get savaged for whatever currently roils the corporate waters.*

I then sat back and watched. Almost always, I saw something swell up inside the five hundred leaders in the audience. They got immersed in the stories, their hearts grew warm, and they left inspired. On those Friday evenings, I saw our values reflected in the hearts and minds of our managers. Their reactions revealed that they had emotionally and psychologically come to identify with the mission and vision of the organization.

The stories reminded them, "This is what we are here to do." The real-life tales reinforced our values. They described how someone had gone the extra mile, put themselves out, poured themselves into a hurting life beyond simply doing their job or working for a paycheck. When these leaders saw the touch of something special on a life, they had more than a physical or emotional reaction. They responded from the heart, with their spirits. And then I knew that *our* values had become *their* values.

Growing a Sound Culture despite Uncertainty

Uncertain times can make even the strongest leader feel at a loss. Sometimes you just don't know what to do. Markets grow volatile. Consumers run this way and that. When your people come to you for reassurance and guidance, be honest with them. Admit that you can't predict with precision what's going to happen.

But despite areas of uncertainty, reassure them that you *can* project certain trends. And so you discuss with your people what those trends could mean. After carefully studying the hard facts, most of the time you can picture at least part of what's coming.

Not too long ago, the Supreme Court of the United States was preparing to hand down a landmark decision about the constitutionality of a big health reform law. Everybody knew that the ruling would have an enormous impact on the future of healthcare in America. But those decisions take time, and we felt like we were just sitting around and waiting.

In my thirty years of working as an executive in healthcare, no one from the Supreme Court has ever called me to give a personal heads-up on the court's final decision. Not once. Of course, any such call would be entirely inappropriate. It would happen only in my imagination.

As I stood before my associates, needing to discuss our future and wanting to lay out what we should do next, I had to face uncertainty. No one knew what the court would decide.

But even in the most uncertain environments, you can point to the good bottom line. You can find performance outcomes in your organization that will win, regardless of how the uncertainties play out. You can say, "Either way, this is what we can do that will help us. Here's what will make us much stronger, more capable of coping with the future, regardless of what happens."

Every good leader needs to become adept at this special kind of defining reality in the face of uncertainty. When you can lay it out clearly, when people feel convinced that you have a good plan, come what may, then the uncertainties of the marketplace don't paralyze the organization. Just hammer away at the certainties.

And so, as we waited for that Supreme Court ruling, I laid out our vision for the next three to five years. I stood up and talked about our strategy. Although we didn't know how the country would finance healthcare or how we would deal with the uninsured, we could continue working on building a better mousetrap. We could become a provider system that delivers better quality at a lower cost. This would help fulfill our mission, no matter how government policies played out. And so we focused on a variety of strategies that could produce a good bottom line. If we succeeded at doing that, then no matter what happened in Washington, we would win. Our values of balance, excellence, and stewardship played a large role in our discussions.

Even if you manage to build a strong organizational culture, however, some of your people will always worry that uncertainties will bring disaster. These Chicken Little folks lose hope and fear a worst-case scenario that will wipe out your organization. By nature, they wring their hands . . . and they can prompt others with a sunnier nature to do the same.

I've found that by focusing on something productive and positive, I can usually get through to them. Admittedly, at times, I've had to put up a hand and stop them. When they kept coming into my office, insisting that the sky was falling, I've even turned to irony: "Could you let me enjoy the little time of peace I have left? Just let me sit here before the end comes."

Gloom and doom will paralyze an organization, and wringing your hands gets in the way of filling out paperwork. So clearly communicate your plan. Tell them forcefully, "We're going to focus on *this*. This will help us out, regardless of our uncertain future. The one thing we're not going to do is sit around, staring at the hazy days ahead."

When your organization faces its own uncertain days, draw on your values to stabilize your culture. Don't allow your own Chicken Littles to cause an epidemic of wringing hands. Treat your worried coworkers with compassion, but point them toward balance. Remind them how responsible stewardship and excellent performance always serve your mission well in any climate. And if your organization has faith-based values, as our company does, fix their wavering hearts on the One who is worthy of all trust, come what may.

In other words, firm up your culture by drawing on the solid values that helped you to build the culture in the first place. When you do that, it's amazing how quickly falling skies can become bright blue once more.

Section Summary

Ten Reasons Values Are Crucial

1. Think of your corporate values as life-saving guardrails that prevent you from driving your company car off a cliff.

2. Organizations that lack a well-defined list of values, or that fail to make them a key part of their culture, are destined for mediocrity.

3. Values are the ambassadors of an organization, a window into your corporate soul. Your values keep your organization safely moving toward your destination.

4. Smart leaders do everything they can to banish mystery from both their organizations and their own leadership styles. Consistently living your values helps eliminate mystery.

5. Relentless stewardship ensures that the use of your resources remains aligned with your mission, vision, and values.

6. Trust is the coin of the realm; when people lose trust in their leader, it's pretty much over. When you consistently demonstrate integrity, you inspire trust and confidence in your brand.

7. No group can become world class without a strong sense of values. The organizational values that you live out reveal what you *really* believe and what you *really* cherish.

8. Values allow others to *see* who you are, but they also help you to remain who you are.

9. Most people won't reach the heart level expressed by a corporate mission until they experience the organization's values every day—primarily in little ways.

10. The values you nurture in the workplace play a critical role in the development of both *meaning* and *hope.*

KEY FOUR

HEALTHY CULTURE

The only thing of real importance that leaders do is to create and manage culture.

— Edgar Schein

In This Section You Will:

- See how an organization's mission + vision + values = its culture.
- Understand why clear boundaries are as crucial in corporations as they are in families.
- Discover five steps in the process of developing a healthy corporate culture.
- Learn how the relentless use of good metrics to evaluate your stewardship will help your organization succeed.
- Discover four guidelines to follow when layoffs become inevitable.

10

Providing Favorable Conditions for Growth

Lessons from a Petri Dish

I BEGAN MY COLLEGE CAREER AS A BIOLOGY major. In the old days, when a professor wanted his students to identify some mystery specimen, he would bring out a collection of test tubes plugged at the top with cotton to protect the cultures inside from contamination. Students then used flame to sterilize a thin little instrument designed to retrieve a bit of whatever oozed inside the tubes. Then they'd remove the cotton plug, reach down into the designated test tube with their freshly sterilized device, remove a bit of the unidentified material, and finally place that recovered substance in a sterile petri dish.

One time, after working all day to reach this critical point in the procedure, I got mixed up. Somehow, I caught a whole rack of cotton plugs on fire. The professor rushed over to me and blew out the raging inferno with a fire extinguisher, destroying my entire day's work. I felt mortified. In fact, my embarrassment at almost catching the lab on fire contributed mightily to my decision soon afterward to switch from chemistry to math.

But before the unfortunate accident occurred, I learned how to grow microscopic bugs in a class called bacteriology. We grew good bugs and nasty bugs and then saw if we could identify them before we killed them.

We grew those bugs in a culture. We called it agar back then, a simple protein bath with all the nutrients necessary to allow our bugs to grow and prosper. Even today, when I think about the word "culture," that's the mental image that comes to mind.

As the CEO of a large organization, I understand that, in many ways, the most critical thing I need to form is a healthy corporate culture. Edgar Schein, a former professor at the MIT Sloan School of Management and the man generally credited with coining the term "corporate culture," even goes so far as to say, "The only thing of real importance that leaders do is to create and manage culture."

The question is *how*. How does a world-class organization create a culture that equips it to fulfill its mission? How does a leader like me get his arms around what it means to grow a healthy organizational culture?

My mind naturally drifts back to those days I spent in college biology class. Can we create an environment, a bath, a set of nutrients around us, in which people grow and flourish in a way that helps us to accomplish the ends of the organization? Can this bath, this culture, motivate us and provide an environment where we find meaning? Can it enable us to reach the point where, out of our own enthusiasm, heart, and passion, we strive to accomplish our organization's mission by pursuing its vision as we uphold its values? Because I know if we can achieve this—if we can build a culture in which our people get up every day, eager to come to work—that then we have created an ecosystem geared for success.

The more I have pondered these questions, the more convinced I have become that the process of growing life in a laboratory test tube or petri dish provides an excellent metaphor for growing a healthy organizational culture. The steps researchers go through in science to create a thriving lab culture have quite a few parallels to how leaders in business and ministry create a healthy organizational culture. In this chapter, I'd like to take you briefly through the process to give you what I hope are some unique insights into this most critical of leadership tasks.

Step 1: Set a Boundary

When you set out to create a culture in a laboratory, you use a petri dish. The wall of the petri dish keeps the culture inside and any contaminants outside. The dish exists, therefore, to create a set of boundaries that make it possible to grow a culture.

Organizations, too, provide boundaries that promote growth. If you want new employees to become emotionally active participants in your organization, then you must create a degree of security for them by providing consistent, caring behavior throughout your organization.

Do your new hires experience such caring behavior from their first day on the job? If they do, then the following day they'll ask themselves, "Did I experience it again?" And over a period of time, if they consistently receive such treatment, they'll start to say, "Hey. No one's going to lie to me here. There's nothing behind the curtain that I don't know about." That creates enormous security.

When you hire someone without a lot of experience, do veterans within your organization help her, especially when she starts to feel overwhelmed? Does she have a manager or experienced colleagues who will reach out to her? Will coworkers willingly extend themselves to offer counsel and advice or reassure her, "Look, I think you're on the right track"? Or instead, does she hear, "Please leave me alone. I don't have time. You need to take care of your own problems"? Does she regularly experience a helpful atmosphere at work, where people care for each other and have each other's backs? Or does she sense a spirit that says, "We're going to hang you out to dry"?

> *Do your people know that you care about them? Does your "speaking the truth" include frequent assurances that you want them to do well?*

What happens the first time a new hire makes a mistake? How does he get treated? Does he experience a redemptive environment, or does he hear, "That's strike one. Two more and you're out"?

Experiences that help someone feel safe create a set of mental boundaries, almost like the physical boundaries of a petri dish. Children who grow up in families with clear and wise boundaries feel safe and secure, while children in boundaryless family environments feel uncertain and anxious, because nothing feels constant to them and nothing makes sense. Everything in their environment looks different to them every day, because they have no boundaries that establish a sense of stability.

Find and use the kinds of leadership metrics that help you to create a healthy culture.

Healthy corporate environments establish clear boundaries, just as healthy families do. Both formal and informal leaders make sure that the values of the organization get lived out around them. They put their arms around newbies and younger employees and help them to understand the group's values. In so doing, they provide living examples of how to live out those values and thereby help everyone to increase their level of job performance, while getting greater work satisfaction at the same time.

It's almost as if caring, considerate behavior produces a force field around those who experience that behavior.

When a cranky employee behaves in an inappropriate way, his healthier coworkers tend to rally around the person who suffered the brunt of the ill behavior, almost as if a force field goes up.

When I talk about these invisible boundaries, I often use the words "security," "honesty," "consistency," and "transparency." And once again, I'm back to the petri dish, because it also has transparent walls. To build a healthy culture, whether in the lab or in your organization, you need boundaries that will allow the culture to grow safely and securely.

Step 2: Provide Favorable Conditions for Growth

A lab culture needs a favorable environment for growth. Sometimes that means light, sometimes it means darkness, it may mean heat, it may mean cooler temperatures. It all depends on what you want to grow. But every healthy culture needs an environment specifically tailored to meet its needs and designed to nurture its growth.

Especially in the last few years, we have given a great deal of thought throughout Adventist Health System to the kind of work environments that will encourage personal, professional, and organizational growth. As we have designed new hospital units, for example, we have thought specifically about things like light, color, and walking distance to nursing supplies. As we implement new forms of automation, we're focused on how to use technology to save time and increase safety. One obvious example is what we call "the closed loop." We have begun using barcoding technology to make it close to impossible for an incorrect drug to be administered to a patient. Technology keeps much better track of this distribution process than human beings can, since rote activity doesn't cause hardware or software to feel a sense of boredom. Automation is *very* good at rote activity. The "closed loop" made possible by the new barcoding technology provides a much safer experience for the patient, but also produces much greater security for the employee.

We're also experimenting with technology to cut down on the amount of time that nurses spend doing documentation. The new systems allow our nurses to use natural language and take advantage of key phrases to develop and track order sets. They can check-box certain phrases rather than laboriously fill out long forms, as required in the past. The new systems not only cut down on overtime, but also give nurses more time to attend to tasks they consider more significant and fulfilling.

The changing demographics of the nation also are prompting us to consider environmental factors that we seldom pondered before. Since nurses often have to work longer hours than in the past, we're looking at the strain on their feet and the design of their shoes and asking what we can do to enable them physically to gain a healthier experience at work. The unfortunate skyrocketing of the nation's obesity rate has led us to equip an increasing number of rooms with lifting equipment so our nurses don't suffer so many injuries from trying to hoist overweight patients, often resulting in the loss of a significant number of workdays.

I tend to group improvements and changes in this arena into two primary categories. First, we are introducing new *tools* to physically help our employees have a more satisfying and enjoyable experience at work. We do this by investing in new technology, developing new processes, and purchasing advanced equipment. Second, we are constantly looking for ways to improve the *psychological* aspects of the work environment, whether that means altering the type or amount of light in a given space, changing the color of a room, improving the décor of an area, or similar enhancements that research shows help us to create a more positive mental state in the workplace. Changes in both categories contribute to a more positive environment in which our organizational culture can grow and thrive.

Leaders who build a culture in which their people are eager to come to work create an ecosystem geared for success.

When I think of environmental enhancements like these, I get excited, because I believe we are on the verge of some phenomenal breakthroughs. Already I have witnessed several notable examples. As patients receive improved care, they feel more secure, more comfortable, and less fearful, and their resulting higher satisfaction levels begin a delightful feedback loop. Happier and more upbeat patients cultivate a less stressed and more buoyant staff, and a more confident and cheerier staff tends to foster even better care. All of this makes for a delightful feedback loop that increasingly benefits both patients and employees.

Step 3: Prepare the Broth

Once you have good boundaries in place and an appropriate environment all ready to go, the next step toward creating a viable culture is to prepare a suitable broth, or solution, in which the culture can grow. The broth, like the environment, must have the right qualities to enable that particular culture to flourish. It must contain essential nutrients designed to sustain the elements that you plan to introduce into the broth. Most of the time that broth is a thick, physical substance impossible to overlook. It's obvious. It's not transparent like the wall of the petri dish. Everybody can see it.

The broth in the scientific world corresponds to the "Big Three" in the organizational world: mission, vision, and values. The solution that enables the lab culture to grow functions in much the same way as does the mix of mission, vision, and values in an organization's culture. In each case, the elements that you place into the broth must find sufficient nourishment in that broth to trigger growth. This analogy once again points out the key importance of taking the time to develop and institute the right combination of mission, vision, and values applicable to your context that will enable your organization to grow. If you get that mix wrong, you will have little chance of creating a healthy, thriving culture.

It is this proper mix of mission, vision, and values that organizations use to try to reach the hearts of their employees and associates. As the leader, you want to challenge them and inspire them so that they *want* to invest the best they have to give of their time, their intellect, their energy, and their creativity to fulfill your collective mission. You want them to move beyond accepting the status quo to looking every day for how you and they, together, can make your organization a better and more effective place to work.

I see some real truth in Maslow's famed hierarchy of human needs. You want to build a culture that encourages your people to go beyond daily values to reach their highest purpose. In this area, leaders and development personnel could all take a cue from one of the greatest leaders of the ancient world. Perhaps you've heard the story of Moses who was raised as a prince of Egypt, spent forty years learning humility as a desert shepherd, then late in life led over a million slaves to freedom. As the massive group of freed slaves approached their destination, Moses gathered the people and gave instructions to parents. He urged them to constantly talk to their children about the preeminent issues of life—when they sit down and rise up, when they walk along the way or enter a room.[14] In other words, parents were encouraged to keep the important issues of life constantly in front of their children—to talk about them frequently, even daily. Continually look for opportunities to reinforce the principles.

By "bathing" children in these ideas, the life lessons had a good chance of sticking with them and influencing the growth and development of future generations.

In similar fashion, as a leader you can keep the higher purpose of your mission constantly in front of your people. And if they see that everyone in your organization, from top to bottom, is getting up every day and coming in and draining the swamp of alligators *because of that higher purpose,* then you'll start to see remarkable things happen. You'll begin to hear of powerful encounters, inspiring meetings, heartwarming interventions, and all sorts of fired-up people going the extra mile and seeing outstanding results. When that starts to happen, you must find some way to stop and reflect on what's taken place, to celebrate it and to extol it. Take the opportunity (it's a golden one!) to reinforce in everyone's minds your group's higher purpose. You tell these stories and gladly recall what happened in order to say to your people, again and again, "This is why we're here. This is why we do this."

Culture is simply the persistent, day-to-day expression of how people tend to behave in an organization.

Maybe you or some of your key people have had two or three bad days in a row. You don't really feel like celebrating. You feel like throwing some telephones through the window. But you stop, reflect, and celebrate anyway, in order to say, "Hey, let's look at what happened. *This* makes it all worthwhile!" Recognitions and celebrations of this kind will produce all sorts of positive energy for you—and that's when your people start moving up Maslow's scale to reach those higher levels and eventual self-actualization. The secret is to keep talking about it. Never stop speaking about it and rehearsing it and celebrating it.

Remember the thickness of the lab culture broth? You create a similar "thickness" and substantive character in your organization through constant repetition. To keep that corporate broth thick and nourishing requires that you constantly keep your mission, vision, and values in front of people. So when something good happens, we say, "Look, here's an example of how this fits in with our mission, vision, and values." And when something happens that doesn't fit into our corporate broth, we can still use it to discuss our mission, vision, and values. Then we say, "Well, it looks like we kind of fell short on that one, didn't we? Okay. Let's come back and do it better the next time." Constant repetition makes your corporate broth thick.

Step 4: Introduce Key Elements into the Broth

What you put into the broth in your lab culture determines what you will grow. Your "inputs" control what your experiment produces. If you put in bacteria, you should not expect to grow yeast. If you put in a virus, you should not expect to grow mold.

The same principle holds true in the creation of your organization's culture. What you put into the "broth" will determine what you grow. In this analogy, the primary input is personnel, whether official leaders, informal leaders, or the rank and file.

We've already looked at the kinds of employees that can make your culture thrive. The 10 percent of your workforce that falls into the "go-getter" category is worth every ounce of effort that you may have to put into it. The 85 percent or so who fall into the "broad middle" can become excellent employees, if given enough training, encouragement, and oversight. And the 2 to 5 percent who qualify as "scoundrels," you need to identify and terminate as quickly as possible.

The key elements in your organizational culture, the ones that generally spell the difference between success and failure, are your leaders. And that includes both your official/supervisory leaders and your informal leaders.

Good leaders always have the pulse of their people. They know what their troops have been going through, and they know what their coworkers need to help them keep moving ahead. I think nearly every day about the folks who work in the stroke units at many of our hospitals. I can't help but marvel at what they go through every week. I remember speaking to the leaders of one of our stroke units and asking them how often they had to deal with the death of a patient. The frequency of loss staggered me. The same thing might be said of those who work on an oncology unit. Doctors, nurses, and support staff tend to get close to their patients over a long period of time, but eventually they lose most of them.

A leader who has the pulse of his or her people continually asks, "What do I need to do today to pick up the morale of my coworkers? How can I encourage them and give them an emotional boost?" In the case of a hospital, maybe at some point the leader calls a chaplain and says, "Could you make it a point to go by this unit for the next few days? Just be available to talk, or to let people talk to you." Or the leader might say to a senior VP, or perhaps to another top administrator, "Listen, these folks are really struggling. I'd appreciate it if you would stop by soon and just give them a pat on the back. They've had a rough four or five days. They've seen a lot of loss and have not been able to catch a break this past week. They need some extra attention right now." Good leaders gauge the pulse of their people and then do whatever it takes to come alongside them and say, "We'll get through this together."

> *When an organization falls short in meeting expectations, it's often the fault of the process and not the people.*

Young CEOs sometimes say to me, "That's fine, Don, but what can I do to make sure I'm putting the right elements into our 'broth'? How can I make sure that we attract the right kind (and the right mix) of supervisors, informal leaders, and workers?"

The first thing I advise is that they pay special attention to who they have in Human Resources (HR) and make sure they have the best training and tools available. I say this because your HR staff are tasked with finding and hiring the best team possible for your company. If they are exceptional at what they do, it has a definite ripple effect throughout the entire company. Many years ago Adventist Health System made some highly focused efforts to beef up HR and become more intentional about who we hired and how we trained. It's night and day compared to what we used to do twenty years ago, and at all levels. In the past, I suppose we just hoped that the right kind of people would find us; but we don't do that anymore. Today we have a long list of things we do to fill our pipeline with both staff level and leadership level people. Testing is a key part of that process. Sophisticated metrics can keep you from making some terrible leadership choices and spare good people from suffering the consequences of your mistakes.

Metrics provide hard data to prove that happy, satisfied workers positively affect your bottom line.

We've also become a lot better at training the leaders we hire. We do a lot more intentional, in-depth training than we ever have before, and it's paying off. If you want to see what may be one of the best examples of what good leadership training can accomplish, I recommend that you consider the United States military. No one trains as relentlessly as it does. It trains its leaders, deploys them, pulls them out again, debriefs them, gives them a respite, trains them some more, and starts the whole cycle all over again. (Full disclosure: I served on active duty as an officer in the United States Navy.)

Not many people realize that in the period between World War I and World War II, the United States had a tiny standing army. It shrank from around two million soldiers at the end of the First World War, to about 140,000 men in uniform for a decade and a half after the war ended. Nobody saw the need for a larger army; imperial Germany and her allies had been defeated, so who could rock the boat?

The one thing the military did right was to keep a much higher ratio of officers to non-commissioned personnel, in the event that the armed forces had to rapidly grow the army for some unforeseen emergency. The military kept in uniform quality leaders who could rise to the occasion, should the need arise. Three or four key individuals in that interwar period had trained under Pershing, and great leaders such as Fox Conner and George Marshall had kept tabs both on the potential stars and the deadwood. When World War II broke out, they immediately cleaned out the deadwood and began promoting several bright young officers—such as George Patton, Dwight Eisenhower, and Omar Bradley—who had been languishing in peacetime and couldn't get a promotion.

Eisenhower had served in the army for a quarter of a century and by 1940 still hadn't made it past the rank of colonel. But once war came to the United States, Marshall tapped Eisenhower for a series of critical jobs, and within about three years he had risen to become a five-star general. It's a great story of leadership and the patient training of someone with outstanding potential.

The US Army published a commemorative brochure about Eisenhower on March 16, 1990, in honor of the former general's one hundredth birthday. It introduced his story by declaring, "In 1941, this remarkable soldier was nearing the end of an undistinguished military career that had afforded him few opportunities to demonstrate his leadership. Yet, within three years and under the intense pressure of a global war, he rose to become Supreme Commander of the Allied Forces in Europe. The leadership skills that won the great land campaigns of the twentieth century did not come about overnight. They were the product of years of development—development that took place in the small peacetime Army of the 1920s and 30s."

Without Eisenhower's patience and the military's thorough training, who knows what might have happened in the dark days following the attack at Pearl Harbor? Never underestimate the value of excellent training.

Still, while training can without question better equip your leaders to create a healthy, thriving culture, I believe that the one indispensable activity, as in everything else, is persistence. You get up and attack it every day. It never ends. You'll never reach the place where you can rightly say, "Whew.

Glad that's done." Just when you think you've got it licked, the next step reminds you of the truth.

Step 5: Remove Toxins

In the lab, occasionally you have to refresh your broth. You take a close look at your culture one day, and something clearly has gone wrong. So you have to replace the old broth with an identical mix of new broth, because waste and toxins have accumulated and spoiled your nice little culture.

The same thing happens in organizations. Toxins accumulate, waste proliferates, and you have to refresh the broth. Unfortunately, it's not as though you get all four steps right and you're done. Growing a healthy culture requires constant work. It's never "done."

Despite all of our leadership testing and staff training, we still find units (medical work groups) populated by actively disengaged people who need to go away. We still encounter managers who need to deal with unhealthy situations but who for some reason just won't. And because they won't do their jobs, they leave their people at the mercy of a force that will do great damage to everyone in those groups. Usually the problem comes down to poor leadership, whether the formal leader or some of the informal leaders, or both.

> *The one indispensable activity is persistence. You never reach the place where you can rightly say, "Whew! Glad that's done."*

If allowed to accumulate, toxins and waste can spoil the most idyllic of cultures. The only remedy is to refresh the broth and introduce new elements . . . and that is the unending job of the leader.

Work Itself Is the Reward

While creating a healthy culture requires extremely hard work, there's almost no feeling like watching the culture you've nurtured grow and thrive and succeed. I've often said that the reward is the work itself.

When you consider the vast amounts of time and effort that you must put in to create a healthy organizational culture, it feels great to look back after decades of exhausting labor and be able to legitimately say, "Would you look at that! I had a part in making that grow."

11

Helping Your People Succeed

Metrics Are Not Just about Better Numbers, but Personal Growth

I KNOW THE TERM "METRICS" SCARES A LOT OF people, especially those who work in the tax-exempt, faith-based world. They often connect metrics with money-grubbing bean counters who want to make life difficult for them. But if they were "Fred" (not his real name), they might have a very different view.

Several years ago, I appointed Fred as the CEO of one of the smaller hospitals in our healthcare system. He had shown a great deal of talent in a vice president role, and the promotion seemed like a logical move. But after no more than a year, it became clear that he struggled with his new position. I began to doubt that, way down deep, he was having a good experience. And clearly, his people had hit a wall. His staff had no energy, I saw lethargy everywhere, and a kind of depression had settled in. Soon I began the painful process of relieving

Fred from his responsibilities.

We provided generous severance, and I made it clear that if Fred wanted to stay within the system, I would give him a strong recommendation for a vice presidential position, but not as a CEO. While I would have wonderful things to say about him as a human being, I could not recommend him as a leader at the highest level. I'm glad to say that Fred went on to work quite successfully for several years as a VP within our system.

But although he dolefully accepted my judgment and followed my counsel, the fact remains that I had put Fred in an untenable position. He did not have the right skill set to succeed as a CEO, and it took me almost a year to see it. My decision to elevate him to that position caused a lot of people a lot of struggles. Fortunately, Fred had the kind of self-acknowledgement, self-esteem, and fundamental mental health to make peace with the demotion and say, "You know, I was really happy when I did VP work. I really enjoyed it. I went home every day feeling pumped. Things were good at work, and they were good at home. That is what I should be doing." But I also have stories of a very different nature. I've had to remove good people from leadership positions who frankly never came to peace with it. To this day, they probably resent me. They wouldn't have one good word to say about me or my decision.

If only there were some way to tell, ahead of time, if a candidate who *looks* like a good fit for some key leadership position *is* a good fit. If only there were a way to avoid putting the Freds of this world into situations that make it far too easy for them to fail.

In fact, there is such a way. And it depends on metrics.

Leadership Metrics: Testing for Success

Today, we have metrics-based tools that would spare Fred, his people, and me a lot of grief. These tools can predict with a high degree of accuracy whether a candidate will succeed at a certain level. They can reveal whether a person will get energized by doing the tasks necessary for a certain job or feel drained and sucked dry by them. The new tools make it much less likely that people like me will make unfortunate decisions when promoting talented candidates to key positions.

If allowed to accumulate, toxins and waste can spoil the most idyllic of cultures.

In the past few years, our organization has picked up serious momentum by formalizing, in a more rigorous way, its senior leadership development process. The testing segment of the process has received special attention. A good cross-section of individuals in each job position has helped us to define various leadership levels. We've laid out the requirements for a system CFO and for a regional hospital CEO, as well as for a chief nursing officer, chief clinical officer, and chief medical officer. We've defined the needed performance metrics in each of those roles. These are not single-dimension positions. Each one requires ability and performance in five to six areas—and all of that can be rigorously defined.

Our testing pulls together certain performance definitions that apply to our specific mission. We can focus, for example, on several things in our environment that our leaders absolutely must be able to do with a high degree of competence. Those things may not apply to other companies, but they do to us, since they take into account our mission and our culture. We evaluate people's ability to help us fulfill our mission and to create the kind of culture that will help our organization to thrive.

This testing keeps us from trying to put a square peg in a round hole. It shows us a person's fundamental makeup. It doesn't necessarily point to something good or bad, and it doesn't point to anything the individual could easily change. It pictures, rather, the way a person is fundamentally wired and shows us whether he or she is disposed to function well in a certain position. In other words, testing doesn't simply weed out people who don't belong in certain positions, it also affirms what really works well in an individual by highlighting his or her strengths.

Most of us in leadership within the Adventist Health System have gone through this process, including me. The results are quite remarkable. I've been tested now for three or four decades, especially regarding my fitness for specific roles. The testing has consistently revealed that what I am as a leader today, I was forty years ago. Although experiences of many types have helped me develop and become much more effective in my role, my fundamental makeup as a leader has not changed, and it won't change. I am where I belong, and I consider it a blessing to have such knowledge.

As we continue to develop this kind of metric-based testing, it becomes increasingly obvious that we (and all companies and organizations) can help our leaders take huge steps forward in their careers. We will place them in positions where they have the best chance to succeed. They will know, going in, the requirements for the position *and that they have the makeup to do the job well.*

No one has precisely the same strengths in every dimension. No human being is a flawless machine. Individuals are stronger in some areas than others. But the testing allows us to see if a person is so weak in any crucial dimension as to undercut his or her ability to handle the job. Ancient Greek heroes often had a fatal flaw that led to a tragic ending. We don't want that kind of story to repeatedly play out here (and you shouldn't in your organization either).

Successful organizations provide boundaries that promote growth.

I expect that, moving forward, I will rarely have to inflict on anyone the sort of conversation I had with Fred so many years ago. The tools we're using now enable me to highlight specific ability issues far more effectively than I could fifteen years ago. I have a high degree of confidence that I'm diagnosing the situation correctly.

Before we developed these testing tools and their precise metrics, it took us quite a long time to get to the heart of the matter with someone. It doesn't take long now. And the best thing about it is that everything can be self-regulating; a person can better evaluate his or her own performance and so not have to rely on others saying, "I wonder if you are a good fit for this job after all?" This becomes increasingly true the higher one rises in leadership.

What we do at Florida Hospital and Adventist Health System in regard to leadership testing, you can do in your own organization. You can use these kinds of leadership metrics to help create a healthy culture that enables you to fulfill your mission and reach your vision. Many such tools exist to help you develop a comprehensive system of testing that fits your organization and its mission, vision, and values.

When you improve your ability to choose the right leaders for the right positions, you will notice an almost immediate improvement in the health of your corporate culture. You can look at the testing data and use it to assist your leaders in their unique tasks. When you make use of these kinds of leadership metrics, you can avoid a lot of unnecessary career crashes and help the Freds in your own organization to find their sweet spots . . . to everyone's great delight.

The Human Side of Metrics

While metrics clearly involve numbers, they're not all about numbers. Metrics provide numbers that can assist us to become better at our jobs, better with other people, better as humans. Many business metrics are explicitly human in nature.

Consider four of the nonfinancial metrics we use constantly. Note especially what they mean to us and how they help us fulfill our mission:

1. Customer service/satisfaction metrics.

It's a simple, incontrovertible fact that your success as an organization depends on satisfying your customers. Unhappy customers do not steer new customers your way.

We've built a strong culture of customer satisfaction by purposefully and regularly seeking out our customers' input and feedback, especially from our patients. We don't ask them to tell us merely how well we performed some medical procedure or how well their nurses treated them. We ask them to be completely honest about everything they liked, everything they didn't like, and how we might better serve future patients.

We employ several methods of gathering customer feedback, including online surveys and "voice of the customer" surveys. These customer service metrics help us measure what we're doing well, what we need to improve, and how our customer satisfaction levels appear to be trending.

Do you measure customer service and satisfaction? Do you know what your customers or clients *really* think of you and your products or services? If you don't, why don't you? What's keeping you from generating the kind of data that can help you to become better at what you're called to do?

2. Customer safety metrics.

Everyone who works in the healthcare industry probably knows about the importance of patient safety, especially as it relates to clinical outcomes (patient survival or improvement in health). We put a major emphasis on patient safety and make sure our people have everything they need to ensure that our patients receive the best care possible.

But this emphasis goes beyond making sure the patient remains safe under our care; it also means we want to ensure that the patient *feels* safe. We understand that a hospital stay can be a stressful, even traumatic, event and that every patient needs to believe we know what we're doing, that we care about the outcome of his or her visit, and that the doctors and nurses and other personnel with whom he or she interacts communicate effectively and work well together.

When your organization faces uncertain days, draw on your values to stabilize your culture.

It's a bit trickier to measure patient safety than it is to measure patient satisfaction, simply because people don't usually think about safety unless something bad happens. For that reason, we continuously conduct surveys throughout our entire organization that seek out our employees' thoughts and feelings about our current culture of patient safety. We ask the people who work for us to give us their honest opinions and observations about our processes as well as the competence of the professionals with whom they work.

If you sell books to the general public or provide career counseling to inner-city youth, you may not think you need to worry about customer safety metrics. And maybe you don't. But have you thought about it? Have you deeply considered whether you could offer a better product or service by paying attention to customer safety metrics? Don't assume they don't apply unless you've pondered the question at length and have concluded that such a metric has no bearing on what you do.

3. Employee satisfaction metrics.

Do you believe that a happy, satisfied workforce is good for business? If so, then you have good intuition. Metrics provide hard data to prove that happy, satisfied workers positively affect your bottom line.

People like to be part of an organization in which they feel valued and important. They want to enjoy their work and their coworkers, and they want to believe that their leaders care about them as individuals and not just as resources.

You can measure employee satisfaction just as readily as you can measure customer satisfaction. Any of several readily available employee satisfaction surveys can give you a good idea of your people's general mood. Gallup is a market leader in such surveys, but you can also find other excellent templates using a quick Google search by using the phrase "employee satisfaction surveys."

Do you know how satisfied and happy your employees

feel at your organization? Do you have a good feel for how their satisfaction, or lack of it, is *right now* impacting your ability to fulfill your mission?

The data from such surveys can help you to focus on making any necessary changes or adjustments within your workplace to improve the corporate culture, resulting in a hike in both employee morale and productivity.

4. Employee engagement metrics.

Employee engagement differs from employee satisfaction in that it measures how committed workers are to their organization's mission, values, and goals, rather than how happy they feel in carrying out their work. An engaged employee truly cares about the mission and values of your organization, and not only about drawing a paycheck. Engaged employees never feel satisfied with meeting minimum performance standards; they consistently go the extra mile to help make the organization great in every way.

Don't you want employees like that? I do.

Employee engagement doesn't mean that the people who work for you feel 100 percent satisfied with everything that goes on within your organization. It simply means that while they acknowledge some things might be done to improve service and further the organization's mission, they believe in what they are doing and are committed to doing it in a way that reflects your stated goals and values.

Do you know your organization's level of employee

engagement? "Well, yes, I talk to employees all the time who tell me how much they enjoy working at a place that has a mission like ours." While anecdotal evidence is great, it doesn't tell you much about the general level of employee engagement within your organization. People who fully engage with your mission and vision will naturally talk about it. But do you *know,* company-wide, how engaged the rank and file is with your stated mission and vision? And if not, don't you think it would be a helpful thing to know?

Defining Reality through Labor Metrics

Labor metrics can be far more problematic for a leader than financial ones, simply because they have to take into account the humanity of those they affect the most. Labor metrics help control labor costs and help give leaders the most "bang for the buck" come payday. Labor metrics include such specifics as units produced per time spent (efficiency), reliability (who routinely shows up for work on time and who often shows up late, as well as who often misses days of work), which departments or positions are prone to high turnover, and many other factors. Labor metrics often make people nervous, because they may affect not only one's paycheck but also the way one does a particular job.

I have found that the vast majority of people need time and persuasion to absorb metrics that indicate a need for change or improvement. The scenario is fairly predictable. After a leader presents the labor metrics, she may say, "Folks, we don't look real good in our labor productivity. We need to take some steps to improve in this area." Immediately, department heads will either protest that they looked better in other metrics, or they'll attack the logic of the metric itself. Or even if they acknowledge the problem, they may retort, "Well, if we had more people and more resources, we would be doing much better."

I've learned to short-circuit such debates by coming to the meeting prepared to shine a little light on the situation. Often, I look beyond simple numbers to study trends. I compare and contrast how a certain department or organization is performing with how it did in the past. If I look at labor productivity metrics and observe that our scores have dropped 25 percent over the previous two years, even though we have worked with the same resources, I know we have an obvious problem on our hands. The numbers help me to clearly define that reality for the people they affect the most.

The key elements in your organizational culture, the ones that generally spell the difference between success and failure, are your leaders.

Benchmarking, when done correctly, can help people to understand the improvements they need to make. Benchmarking answers performance-oriented questions such as "according to whom" or "compared to what?" It allows us to look at a host of institutions or departments of the same size or type that are doing the same kind of work and objectively declare, “We’re in the bottom quartile”—meaning that 75 percent of the institutions or departments doing the same kind and same volume of work we do are more productive than we are.

In one hospital I led, we took a systematic look at each department to evaluate our corporate performance. When we applied standard benchmarks, we found that the radiology department had a great deal of room for improvement. It didn’t have close to the number of scans it should have had, based on the work-hours it reported. So I sat down with the head of the department and laid out the numbers. He did not react well. At first, he got a little flustered and fumbled with several reasons why his department couldn’t match the standard.

While a culture can become diseased rather quickly, it takes a very long time to build a strong, healthy one.

So I laid out the facts again. I explained the studies of radiology departments all over the country—with the same tasks to perform and the same resources at their disposal as his department—that boasted far better numbers. I explained that he needed to figure out how to change things in his department so he could approach those numbers.

He grew very silent, then after a moment, replied, “Well, I’m just not going to do that.”

I had a high regard for this staff member. He wasn't some slacker trying to get by on the minimum; he had always taken his responsibilities seriously. But for some reason, he resisted the numbers and rejected my direction.

I very calmly replied, "Okay, if you're telling me that you're really not going to do it, then that probably means you need to look for another job." He grew a little pale, but I continued: "If you're telling me you don't know *how* to do it, then that's different. Here's my suggestion. Take some time on your own, consider what you might do to achieve the required improvement, and then I'll work with you on how to close the gap."

As he sat there in silence, trying to take in this new directive, I told him of a discovery I'd made recently while walking around the hospital. "In your department," I said, "you have a group of staff that clocks in at seven every morning. The first thing they do is go to the cafeteria and have a forty-five-minute breakfast—on my time."

A stunned look crossed his face. He couldn't believe I knew such details.

"The problem is," I continued, "their eight hours are up at three in the afternoon, but the majority of your patients come in for scans in the late afternoon. And so these staff members stay overtime to do the scans. And that's overtime I really shouldn't be paying."

He slowly nodded his head in agreement. "Yeah, that's not appropriate."

I described some radiology departments in nearby hospitals, virtually identical to his own in size and patient volume but which had better performance. I said that I would pay him to study those facilities, evaluate their procedures, and develop some ideas for improving his department's production. In time, this man came around, made the adjustments, and did a great job of bringing his department up to industry standards.

It's possible to help an entire department improve by using metrics—even when, at first, managers want to turn their backs on them. And you do this by making the numbers both tangible and reachable.

Using Metrics to Motivate

Experience has taught me that when an organization falls short in meeting expectations, it's often the fault of the process and not the people. When you or your managers continually hammer on the wrong things or focus on certain people, you run the risk of exacerbating the situation by further damaging employee satisfaction.

I have found that I can provide the energy our organization needs by stressing the idea of growth—personal growth and organizational growth. Most individuals want to succeed and long to be part of a successful organization. Who doesn't want to be a winner? And who doesn't want to be part of an organization whose culture gives them the opportunity to excel at what they do?

You will find it much easier to motivate your people once they know you're serious when you say, "I want this organization to grow and succeed, and I want everyone who works here to do the same." That's the most important factor in defining performance through metrics. Your employees need to believe in their hearts that it's not just about you wanting better numbers but that it's about their growth.

Do your people know that you care about them? Does your "speaking the truth" include frequent assurances that you want them to do well?

I always try to have credible, believable performance metrics with me and to base our conversation on those facts. I define what a good department does and challenge people to think with me about how to get there. They know I want them to do well and that I don't use the numbers to beat them over their heads.

Don't shortchange reality, but make it clear that you will do everything in your power to help your people succeed. You'll coach, you'll teach, you'll find resources, you'll walk them through the necessary steps to achieve better performance.

Whatever the area of expertise of those reporting to you, you can appeal to their desire for success. No one wants to fail. Find a way to cast better performance in a positive light. When you give them a picture of a better way to do things, almost everyone will respond positively.

Use Metrics to Keep on Track with Mission

This bears repeating: Always view whatever metrics you employ through the lens of your mission and vision.

At Adventist Health System, we use metrics not only to help us utilize our financial resources more efficiently but also to improve the service we provide to everyone who comes through our doors for medical treatment. We know we haven't "arrived," and in one respect we know we never will. Even if we reach the top decile in every area of service, we'll never get to a point where we believe we can't get even better.

That kind of striving for continual improvement can create its own struggles. When we receive high marks for our patient service or when our clinical outcomes beat the industry, it's possible that we can look at our achievements and think we've become the best we can possibly be. But that can become an excuse for complacency.

How do you balance legitimate pride with foolish self-satisfaction? It's a never-ending challenge.

When I first arrived as CEO of one of our particularly successful hospitals in Adventist Health System, I saw an air of pride—maybe even arrogance—over what the organization had accomplished. In many respects, this hospital had already become a truly great healthcare organization. But I also saw that it tended to overlook areas where it didn't have great performance, services where it needed genuine improvement.

In a way, we could call this "the dark side of metrics."

Excellence in healthcare, like excellence in your own industry, is a constantly moving target. What we consider great today could get ridiculed in another year or two (if not sooner). And that is why we so relentlessly use metrics to evaluate and reevaluate our performance. We use metrics to make sure our patients feel well cared for and happy with the treatment they receive, and we use metrics to improve our employees' satisfaction with their work environment.

Why do we do this? We do it because we want to be a world class healthcare provider. And because we want to stay there.

What would it mean for you to become world class in your own industry?

12

Changing an Unhealthy Culture

Don't Cut Off the Dog's Tail One Inch at a Time

LIFE BRINGS CHANGE, AND NOT ALL OF THOSE changes bring better health. When you step on the scale one morning to see a figure about forty numbers higher than you had hoped for, that represents an unhealthy change that you simply cannot afford to ignore.

Life brings changes to organizations, too, and some of them sneak up on you. Whether they happen gradually or occur almost overnight, however, you have to address them forcefully. Regardless of the challenge—financial trouble, an attitude problem, a loss of focus, a shifting business landscape, or some other negative change in your organization—you as the leader have to step in and tackle whatever threatens your corporate health.

And by "tackle" I do not have in mind the response of too many leaders who cave in to pressure from well-meaning colleagues and associates. Through all of my management life, individuals have approached me with some problem that needed fixing. And their first impulse, almost without exception, is to ask me to throw money at it. You can probably imagine my reaction. Such a wrongheaded but common strategy builds layer upon unproductive layer of ineffective processes that make it hard for an organization to succeed.

Be Clear and Prepared

Whether you need to tweak something in your organization in order to nurse it back to health, or you have to perform radical surgery to save the patient's life, make sure that your actions line up with your mission. Let your organizational mission guide everything you do. Too many executives feel tempted to jettison it, imagining themselves as benevolent dictators who have to impose martial law in order to bring order to the chaos.

Your mission, however, is your greatest asset. When you can point to your mission as the reason behind the changes you need to make, your job becomes much less difficult. Most people eventually will see that the fulfillment of your unchanging mission requires these changes. And if you don't help them to see this, it will look to them as though some rogue administrator with delusions of grandeur has taken power.

Here's one illustration that demonstrates how important is it to be clear about your organization's mission so that you can apply it wisely and avoid others' misuse of it.

Many years ago, I had to lay off a lot of employees in order to save a teetering institution. A powerful church leader whose sister had lost her job in the layoff told me angrily, "Don't you know that the mission of Christian hospitals is to provide employment for Christians?"

"Well," I replied, "I have my mission statement right here in front of me, and let me tell you how it reads. My mission is not to provide employment to anyone, but to extend the healing ministry of Christ. Now I certainly love to hire rightly motivated church members because they can be a wonderful asset to our mission, but hiring them is not the mission of our hospital." He eventually cooled down when he saw that I had acted in line with our mission and not against it.

I hope you can handle such a situation more diplomatically than I did, but whatever you do, don't let yourself get muddled and confused about your mission. Stay clear on it and help everyone else to remain equally as clear. You may not have angry church members questioning your mission as I did, but regardless of what your organization's mission is, you will likely have people challenge your decisions based on their perception of your mission. So be clear and prepared.

Also, don't be unrealistic about the amount of time it takes for changes to cure a sick corporate culture. If you are trying to bring some significant adjustments to your organization, you can count on a minimum of three years until the changes become irreversible. If you need to bring some *really* big and complex modifications to your culture, you're probably looking at closer to five years.

I've known leaders who ran out there, did something radical, and to their great delight, saw some hopeful signs in the first six months. So they let up. But they soon discovered that culture is like a rubber band: without a long-term approach, it will bounce back to its former state. In unhealthy cultures, particularly those that involve long-time managers and employees with dysfunctional habits, some of your people will try to wait you out. They hope you will go away or that the changes will go away. Permanent change will not come to your culture until these individuals either move out of the organization or the pain of resistance finally prompts them to get on board. Lasting change will not come to your organization's culture until everyone gets it clear: *This is not going away.*

> *Entire departments can improve by using metrics when you make the numbers both tangible and reachable.*

And remember, the best ally you have in bringing such a conviction to their hearts is your unbending commitment to your organization's mission. You have to convince everyone that you're taking these painful actions *because* of the mission you all love. It is *because* of that mission that neither you nor the new directives are going away.

Small Adjustments Now Can Prevent Big Changes Later

It's always best, of course, if you don't have to make major changes to bring your organization back to health. And most of the time, you can avoid dire situations and radical adjustments simply by remaining disciplined, focused, and vigilant. If you keep on top of the situation and work every day to sustain a healthy culture, then usually you can avoid massive layoffs and profound course corrections.

Do you honestly know what your customers or clients really think of you and your products or services? If you don't, why don't you?

A significant part of such vigilance is to remain disciplined about annual employee evaluations. Never get lax about divesting yourself of the Scoundrels and the actively disengaged who inevitably wind up in your organization. Make sure you're continually keeping an eye on this critical segment of your culture's health.

In regard to underperforming employees, by contrast, I tend to move a bit more slowly. Since I want to give everyone an ample chance to succeed, we try to do everything we can to help our people perform up to expectations. I see this as one area of legitimate difference between tax-exempt groups and for-profit corporations. It's not a difference in discipline or diligence, but a difference in aggressiveness. Tax-exempt organizations can legitimately exercise a bit more patience with employees than for-profits generally do—not that we will tolerate poor performance, but we can usually grant a little more time for the person to "get it right."

The tax-exempt may choose to go the extra mile, while the aggressive for-profit usually won't go the extra foot. In our kind of tax-exempt organization, we would rather err by moving a little bit late . . . but not so late as to damage the organization. When I ask myself, "Did I give this person every chance to succeed?" I want the answer to be "yes."

If it becomes clear, for any number of reasons, that you must trim your staff, look wherever possible to attrition as a means of labor cost control. At least nine times out of ten, you should be able to make appropriate adjustments to labor costs through attrition. And that's attrition across the board, not just to low-profile areas. Look at *everything,* including top management. If you bring decisions about replacement to the highest level of management, people will tend to bring forward only the critical positions. Your willingness to include upper management in these decisions sends a signal to the whole organization that you're serious about getting your organization back to solid health.

When Layoffs Have to Come

Sometimes, unfortunately, situations overtake you and give you no choice but to do a true layoff. Maybe twenty things hit all at once, and now you must immediately reduce the size of your workforce. Let me suggest four guidelines to help you manage this admittedly unwelcome process:

1. Keep your administrative staff lean.

If people in your organization perceive that you always try to keep overhead down and that you keep your administrative staff lean and mean, you defuse a lot of institutional anger. While nothing about this process is easy, your people are certain to react badly if they see your administration becoming top heavy. Keep it as lean as you can get it. I would rather be a little understaffed in senior management than overstaffed.

A lean organization tends to communicate more effectively and respond more nimbly than a top-heavy one. If your administration gets too complex with too many layers, you cause yourself a host of unnecessary problems.

Frequently it makes good sense to get your executives to wear more than one administrative hat and so benefit the organization in some unexpected ways. In a smaller to medium-sized organization, your vice presidents and administrative staff will have to cover more departments and areas of responsibility than they would in a larger organization where specialization rules. This can become a real positive for those who aspire to become a CEO, because they must become adept at managing a broad number of things. It can highly motivate these individuals, because they gain valuable experience for their career path, since a CEO is always the greatest generalist in the organization.

It also means these organizations have fewer "silos." Because the team is smaller, the team-building fostered by the CEO can become more effective. The smaller the family, the closer it can grow, which engenders better mutual support and tighter communication. As a result, fewer silos get created.

In an organization with a flatter and leaner administrative team, decisions also get made faster. Real problems get communicated higher up the chain more quickly and therefore can be resolved faster—something both employees and directors notice. The CEO remains closer to the action because he or she has to work through fewer layers.

2. Assess your core staffing needs.

Make sure you know your core staffing needs. What essential personnel must you have in order to keep running your operation? Some groups operate so close to their core staffing needs that when their income drops, even a little, they find themselves in real trouble. They simply have no room to flex. Try hard not to be such an organization.

3. Use a small team to make critical staffing decisions.

Few people are good at keeping secrets. Winston Churchill is credited with saying, "Two people can keep a secret if one of them is dead." When you have to discuss which employees stay and which must go, your deliberations must remain discreet. Without such confidentiality, you risk inflicting a lot of damage and even trauma on your organization.

I think it best to discuss any potential layoffs with a small group of four or five individuals, probably just your top management staff, perhaps vice presidents and above. Have careful, quiet deliberations about what you need to do to arrive at exactly how many and which employees you must remove. This must be done with utmost confidentiality. Holding any such discussion in the open will lead to the whole organization worrying and agonizing—an excellent way to destroy the very thing you are trying to save.

Gather a small, select group of people to discuss confidentially *exactly* what you need to accomplish. If some in the organization complain about your secret deliberations, let them complain. Continue to do your work, knowing that the health and perhaps even the existence of your organization are at stake.

4. Identify the specific criteria that you will use.

Before you do anything, look at the demographic profile of your organization. Make sure that it won't look dramatically different after the layoff than before it. Consider carefully such factors as age, gender, and ethnicity. Your cuts must not appear to discriminate against any particular group of employees or you may violate important legal protections. So before you allow anyone to pull the trigger on any layoffs, take a snapshot of your current demographics to make sure they don't look significantly different in a post-layoff snapshot. Take care to avoid unintentionally skewing that mix in any way, shape, or form.

Seniority also will play a role in your deliberations. I do not like making layoff decisions solely on the basis of seniority. I usually prefer to use a mixed criterion of seniority and performance. My general principle is to honor seniority, except where a clear performance difference exists. If we have two people who perform with equal excellence, then we lay off the junior person; but if the junior person clearly has better performance, then the one with seniority is let go. When we finish, we want an organization superior to what we had before.

For leaders, there's almost no feeling like watching the culture you've nurtured grow and thrive and succeed.

When I had to lead layoff discussions at one hospital, everyone outside of our leadership team assumed we would make our decisions strictly on the basis of seniority. In the nursing ranks, particularly, some units had long-time employees whom everyone recognized as chronic problems. Over a period of a week or so, we deliberated over a list of people who might lose their jobs. I carefully went over every name. Finally I said to the group, "Okay, we have our list."

A couple of days after we informed the affected individuals and word had spread about who had been laid off, a nurse came up to me in a community event and said, "I never in a thousand years dreamed that you would lay off that individual. I didn't think anyone would take care of that problem." I just smiled.

Those kinds of decisions send an inordinately powerful message throughout the organization, namely, that you have no "untouchables" among you. As difficult as these decisions can be, I consider them almost a godsend because they provide tremendous help in changing an unhealthy culture. I can't overstate their significance.

If you have "untouchables" in your organization and your people perceive that these protected individuals can do anything they want to do without consequences, then the morale in your organization will plummet. Make it clear that, from your perspective as the leader, you have *no* untouchables within your organization. Any organization that allows untouchables to exist deserves to fail, starting with the CEO.

Never Cut Off the Dog's Tail One Inch at a Time

One of my philosophies is *never cut off the dog's tail one inch at a time.* If you have to go for a layoff, go deep enough that you can, with a high degree of confidence, face the remaining employees and with a straight face tell them, "This is over, done. We've taken care of what we needed to do. We've put it behind us. We are over with it."

Do it all quickly and get it behind you. This makes it easier on everyone, even those who lose their jobs, because they can get away, be by themselves, and process the loss. You reduce the trauma felt by both those who stay and those who must leave.

For the organization, it's not a good thing to say, "We have to go through this long, drawn-out process. We're very sorry, but we must do it this way. We regret this has happened to you; why don't you work another week and then be gone?" What a horrible thing to do! It's bad for everybody. Think about the employees still there. In our case, many have critically ill patients to take care of. They must be able to focus on the work at hand.

Go deep enough with your cuts so that you greatly reduce the chances of having to do it again, anytime soon. Help your employees to feel as secure as possible so that they can move forward and get on with the business at hand.

If you are trying to bring some significant adjustments to your organization, count on a minimum of three years until the changes become irreversible.

When a hospital that I served had to go through a significant layoff, we worked hard to get it all announced and done in a single day. I walked through the facility, announcing who was going to be terminated, giving them their benefits and saying, "Thank you very much for your service." I hated it. It felt very, very painful. Everyone who lost their job was asked to leave the campus by the end of that day.

"That sounds awfully harsh and cold," someone says. And on the surface, I agree. But think it through and you may see the wisdom in it. We laid off about forty people that day, and within about two months, every one of them found new employment somewhere else. Those who remained could get on with life and do their jobs without wondering when and where the axe might fall next. We told our people, "We're done with the cuts. We believe we can make this work as we move ahead." Within about two weeks, there was an incredible positive energy surge through the entire organization.

Don't Be Cruel

When you must go through a layoff, make it as easy on people as you can. Think about anything and everything you can do to protect the dignity of each person affected. It's almost always true that the individuals laid off didn't "have it coming." So you can truthfully say, "This is not about you. Although this clearly affects you and we're very sorry it has come to this, what has happened is not about your performance. This is not about you as a person. It's just that the organization has gotten itself into a difficult place where it has to make these adjustments." Do whatever you can to show genuine compassion.

That includes being as generous as possible. Although a major layoff probably means that your finances have taken a hit, be as generous as possible with severance packages. Think about the process as if you were on the other side of the table. How would you want this to be handled if you were the one getting laid off? Whatever you can think of to make it as easy as possible, do it that way. For example, I think it's horrible to do a layoff three days before Christmas or on a Friday. Don't mess up someone's weekend! If it must be done, do it early in the week. I typically have picked Mondays.

Be honest with everyone and avoid saying things like, "This hurts me more than it does you." My mother once spoke those very words to me just before she gave me a spanking. It might have been true, but I hated it. *Hey,* I thought, *I'm the one that's getting walloped here! What do you mean, this hurts you more than me?* Such words, regardless of their kind intent, don't go down well at such a painful time. So speak about the affected person and not about yourself. And if you have counselors or chaplains, make them available. In general, be as compassionate as you are honest. Put yourself in the other's place.

Since in most situations I can't communicate with every affected person in a single day, I spent a lot of time training my managers and other leaders how to communicate the sad news. We role-modeled the process and said, "This is how you will communicate our decision. You will do it exactly like this." We trained everyone to deliver the news in the very same way.

None of this makes it any fun, of course. I'd be very happy if I never had to do anything like it again. But if you're the leader, it goes with the territory. Just get prepared for what may follow.

Face the Ugly Music

Once you become the leader, you must be willing to make difficult calls and hard decisions and deal with what hurt and frightened people might say about you or to you. You also must be willing to accept your own fallibility, because you won't get everything right.

I remember one instance where I had become convinced that a particular person couldn't do his job well. So I made a change, the person left our organization, and soon became very successful somewhere else. In that case I had to be willing to admit, "Maybe I got it wrong on that one."

> *If your values are right and consistent with your mission, and the people within your organization live out those values most of the time, then by definition you have a healthy culture.*

You also must learn to deal with fury vented in your direction. Anytime that you make a significant personnel change, especially if it concerns a direct report and disciplinary action, expect a highly unpleasant reaction. Think about it carefully ahead of time and try to anticipate the reaction and the outcome, based on your knowledge of the person and your estimation of the way the relationship has gone in the past.

Most of the time, I like to handle these situations privately and discreetly. When I have suspected the situation might become really ugly and nasty, I have asked a witness to be present. At other times, I've handled the initial termination news but then turned to a trusted attorney to negotiate specific separation issues. I've retained lawyers because at least the attorney hadn't made the decision or delivered the news, and I thought the interchange might be less volatile and contentious. I've also done it this way because I wanted to protect the organization against potential litigation. I wanted the right person with the right skill set to handle things.

If you sit in the leader's chair, count on it, you will make some people angry. They will insult you, call you bad names, and sometimes threaten you. That's just the way it is. That's life as a leader. And it can't be helped. It's part of what you sign up for when you become a leader. But there is something worse. If you are unwilling to make the tough calls that a leader must sometimes make because you don't want to upset people, then you will likely be doing your company a disservice and probably steering it toward mediocrity at best and disaster at worst.

The Emotional Toll

I say, "It can't be helped," but that may make it sound as though angry encounters never dent the armor of a successful leader. Any such impression lies. My own armor shows not only very large dents, but creases, chinks, and holes.

Make no mistake, serving as the leader in a time of forced change can take a huge emotional toll on you. I have no idea how much these painful times have shortened my own life, but I'm quite sure they have done so. I've had to shut down businesses, sell off hospitals, lay off hundreds of upstanding human beings. I wonder if some of my own health issues have arisen, or at least grown worse, from the emotional wear and tear of those old battles. Please, don't ignore the emotional toll that leadership can take.

Years ago I read a book on military history that discussed the emotional strain of wartime command on three kinds of generals. I've long since forgotten the title, but it sketched out how each sort of commander dealt with sending men into deadly combat. General A strategizes how to take a hill or defeat a heavily entrenched enemy, and although he knows many of his men won't survive, he doesn't lose any sleep over the coming death toll. General C, by contrast, can create an effective battle plan, but the idea of sending hundreds of men to their deaths keeps him from pulling the trigger; he cannot live with the consequences. And General B, emotionally between his two colleagues, can develop effective tactics that accomplish his objective while minimizing losses. He'll agonize over every death . . . but he'll move ahead anyway.

If you're the president, which general do you want in charge?

You can't choose General C, because he'll lose the war. You might choose General A for some urgent situations, but you won't put him in charge of everything; you have more compassion on the nation's mothers than that. In most situations, you'll rather call on General B. He'll get the job done with as few casualties as possible.

Of course, General B also will end up with more emotional baggage than either General A or General C. Leadership takes an emotional toll, no question about it . . . but that's also no reason not to lead.

No Silver Bullet

I don't know of any leader who enjoys the process of "making over" an unhealthy organizational culture. While I have felt a great deal of satisfaction in pulling an organization back from the brink, I haven't had any fun in doing so.

If your turn should come, manage it as compassionately as possible and do everything in your power to remake the culture in a way that seeks to protect everyone's dignity. But don't kid yourself: There's no magical silver bullet about how to do this without tears.

I've thought about this painful issue a great deal. And I must tell you that one of the things I'm most looking forward to about heaven is never having to worry about it again.

Changing an unhealthy culture may be difficult, but with courage, compassion, and a solid grasp of your company's mission, vision, and values, it can be done effectively—and when that happens it will bring new life to your future.

Section Summary

Ten Important Ideas Related to Your Company Culture

1. As a leader, one of your most critical tasks is to form a healthy company culture. Leaders who build a culture in which their people are eager to come to work create an ecosystem geared for success.

2. You know you're creating a healthy culture when your mission is communicated every day—throughout your organization—in little, but practical displays of your values.

3. To create a healthy culture, whether in the research lab or in your organization, you need both a *vibrant environment* and *well-defined boundaries* that will allow the culture to grow safely and securely.

4. Culture is like a rubber band; without a long-term approach that stretches your team, it will spring back to its former state.

5. You want to build a culture that encourages your people to reach their highest purpose. Metrics can assist you to become better at your job, better with other people, better as a human being.

6. The single most important factor to grasp about metrics is this: Metrics are not just about you (or any leader) wanting better numbers. Employees must know and believe in their hearts that metrics are about their personal growth and success. For when they measurably grow and succeed, the organization does as well.

7. Do your people know that you care about them? Does your "speaking the truth" include frequent assurances that you want them to do well?

8. Always view whatever metrics you employ through the lens of your mission and vision, with your commitment to relentless stewardship keeping everything in focus.

9. A lean organization tends to communicate more effectively and respond more nimbly than a top-heavy one.

10. If your values are right and consistent with your mission, and the people within your organization live out those values most of the time, then by definition you have a healthy culture.

KEY FIVE

OUTSTANDING LEADERSHIP

Our business in life is not to get ahead of other people, but to get ahead of ourselves.

— Maltbie D. Matlock

IN THIS SECTION YOU WILL:

- See how to turn criticism into something beneficial—for yourself and the group you serve.
- Learn how your organization's mission statement can function as "armor" for yourself and your leadership team.
- Understand why trying to please everyone can derail your practice of relentless stewardship.
- Realize why your vital first step as a leader is to face reality, and to help others in your organization do so as well.
- Remember four sources of support you can call upon when you have become the target of hurtful criticism.

13

Put On Your Armor

How to Survive and Even Thrive amid Criticism

IF OUR NATION'S ELECTED LEADERS KNOW anything well, it's that they will face criticism. Our system of government allows for debate, which sometimes grows intense. Consensus often doesn't come easily. Consequently, our leaders get criticized a lot, from both the left and from the right, fairly and unfairly, openly and secretly.

As someone once said, "If you want a friend in Washington, get a dog."

Abraham Lincoln, who led our nation during some of its darkest days, continually felt the sting of criticism—relentless, brutal criticism, probably the worst any US president has ever faced. He expected much of it, since he presided over the split between the North and the South. The American Civil War claimed more than 600,000 American lives and untold numbers of wounded.

As the 1864 US presidential election approached, many questioned whether Lincoln could win. The American people had suffered through three years of horrific fighting between the forces, when nearly everyone had thought the war would last only weeks. Grief over mounting losses and fear for the future gripped the hearts of many voters, making Lincoln extremely vulnerable to defeat.

At one point, a Union Army officer approached Lincoln and suggested that he respond to some ruthless criticism regarding his conduct of the war. But Lincoln steadfastly refused. He said:

> If I were to try to read, much less answer, all the attacks made on me, this shop might as well be closed for any other business. I do the very best I know how—the very best I can; and I mean to keep doing so until the end. If the end brings me out all right, what's said against me won't amount to anything. If the end brings me out wrong, ten angels swearing I was right would make no difference.[15]

I had that quotation framed and hanging in my office, although eventually I took it down. I didn't want people to think I disregarded criticism or that I would dismiss their legitimate concerns about how I handled my work. Still, I love that quotation. In many ways, it embodies what I see as a sound, healthy attitude toward criticism.

Don't Take It Personally

Leadership isn't for the weak of heart. Neither is it for the thin skinned. As the leader of your organization, you will have to make lots of tough decisions on a slew of critical issues.

And not everyone will agree with every decision you make.

Every person in the world has his or her own ideas about how things should be done, and some have their own skin in the game. More than a few of those you lead will offer their criticisms of how you do your job. Some may want you to implement your decisions in a slightly different way, while others may loudly complain that your decisions will surely send your organization straight off the deep end.

Unless you have some kind of masochistic streak, you don't consider any criticism "fun." When someone criticizes you or something you've done, it feels like an attack. And while your critics may not intend for it to seem personal, it often feels exactly that way.

I've observed that leaders get criticized primarily on one of three factors:

1. Their ability
2. Their behavior
3. Their motives

None of us likes criticism of our ability or behavior, though often we can learn from it. But criticism of our motives can cause us excruciating pain, because that kind of criticism goes to the very roots of who we are. It's personal by its very nature.

When someone calls my motives into question, they're criticizing what's on my heart and calling into question my personal character—and an attack like that can feel utterly devastating.

Leaders, too, can lob this sort of inappropriate criticism at others. In fact, we may have an even greater tendency to do so, simply because fewer people will dare to call us on it. So let me say this bluntly: Leaders who question the motives of their employees or colleagues, whether publicly or privately, risk destroying not only the object of that criticism but also their ability to influence and work with others.

Leadership isn't for the weak of heart or for the thin-skinned.

We have a hard enough time sorting out what lies hidden in the dark recesses of our own hearts, let alone judging the secrets buried in the hearts of others. So I try to follow the wise counsel of an extraordinarily successful leader from long ago: "Don't judge others, and you will not be judged. Don't accuse others of being guilty, and you will not be accused of being guilty. Forgive, and you will be forgiven."[16]

Avoid criticizing the motives of others. And when someone criticizes your motives, try to remember that they know the contents of your heart even less than you do.

How, though, should you respond to criticism of

your ability or behavior? First and foremost, don't take it personally. Listen carefully for any kernel of truth you might find. And whatever you do, don't dismiss it out of hand because you don't like how it makes you feel.

I recently heard about the leader of an internationally known tax-exempt ministry who responded to criticism by taking it personally. The criticism made him feel uncomfortable, and therefore he immediately labeled it as off base and irrelevant . . . and the ministry suffered because of his failure to consider legitimate criticism.

Employees within this organization had expressed general discontent over how certain kinds of staff situations tended to get handled. This leader wisely wanted to take some practical steps to deal with such problems, and so he commissioned an outside firm to conduct a survey of his mid-level and upper-level managers. Each of these managers anonymously answered the survey questions. When the results came back, it became apparent that the problems started at the very top. Words and phrases such as "autocratic," "self-impressed," "pompous," "won't listen to others," and "overly demanding" appeared repeatedly in the results.

The next time your leadership is criticized, listen closely to the concerns being voiced. Ask clarifying questions. Ask what you can do to perform better.

When the group's leadership met to discuss the survey, this leader stood up before his managers and proclaimed, "This is not me. End of story," and then moved on to the next item on the agenda. As you might guess, nothing changed. As a result, many good people left the organization.

In this leader's case, his direct reports and managers never criticized his ability or his motives, just his behavior. And while the problems listed in the survey results were all fixable, this leader made real change impossible by taking the results personally: *This is not me.*

Taking criticism personally will put you on a sure path to preventing needed changes from occurring. It will ensure that the people in your organization will hesitate to talk to you honestly about their concerns. And it will keep discussion on a surface level that never gets to the core. None of these things will benefit an organization, regardless of its size; in fact, they may spell the end of what could have been an amazing endeavor.

Wise leaders look for whatever truth they can find in the criticism directed their way. Taking it personally only stunts personal and organizational growth. If you want to lead well, then learn to weigh criticism dispassionately and without taking it personally.

The Leader's Armor

Every leader gets criticized. Count on it. If you want to survive the criticism and even use it for your benefit, then learn to approach it in the context of your organization's mission. When you constantly make decisions according to what you see as the best way to help your organization fulfill its mission, then in effect, you're strapping on the armor of the "high moral ground" to protect yourself from the slings and arrows of unjustified criticism.

In my role of leading leaders, I do everything I can to emphasize the importance of spending time in deep thought about our organization's mission and about how we can explain our decisions in the context of our mission. I stress the importance of being able to explain why we do what we do, in the case of Adventist Health System, that we might extend the healing ministry of Christ. Whatever the mission is of your organization, you can do the same.

Leaders who question the motives of their employees or colleagues risk destroying their ability to work with others.

Such a practice serves as the leader's armor. I don't knowingly let any of my leaders go into battle for a single day without putting on that armor.

Think about the definition of the word "armor." Literal armor serves as a defensive weapon, a covering that protects the warrior from weapons of offense, such as spears, arrows, or bullets. When a leader puts on the armor of her organization's mission, that leader no longer needs to feel so vulnerable to criticism and no longer needs to take criticism so personally, because the mission itself serves as her protection.

I find it far easier to make tough decisions when I take care that each of them helps our organization fulfill our mission. When I put my decision-making process through this grid, critics find it far more difficult to claim that I reached some decision based on merely personal interest or a raw display of power. When I get criticized for some decision, I first explain that we operate under a mission and a corresponding set of values, and that in everything we do, we look for the moral high ground. I then do my best to explain why I and other leaders believe that the decision we've made most effectively helps to fulfill our mission.

The best advice I can give about handling criticism without taking it personally is this: *Get a rock-solid understanding of your mission and then practice explaining how your decisions enable your organization to further its mission.* In other words, put on your armor. Then you'll handle criticism in a way that strengthens your organization. In fact, you might even find yourself beginning to welcome criticism.

Criticism and Accountability

When I first heard of the problems plaguing the prominent ministry described earlier in this chapter, it occurred to me that this organization lacked one important element: accountability. Think for a moment about the scenario. The head of a well-known, international ministry hires an outside firm to survey his managers, and when the results of the survey rankle him, he simply dismisses them. *End of story.*

I have a hard time believing that this ministry has a strong and effective board of directors that holds its leadership accountable or gives the organization the essential oversight it needs. In other words, this organization likely has become more like a monarchy than a ministry, with a man at the top who functions more as a ruler than a leader. Monarchies operate largely without any accountability. And without accountability, an organization inevitably either gets stuck in a deep rut or implodes. No organization can move forward and effectively fulfill its mission statement without accountability. Think of legitimate criticism as a form of helpful accountability.

In the world of healthcare—processes, technology, and financial structures are constantly changing (often improving), and what five years ago was considered world class, nobody considers world class today. Good, efficient healthcare is a constantly moving target, and those of us who work within that world understand that we must actively seek out criticism and input if we intend to grow and adapt. And so we relentlessly seek it out as another form of accountability.

My organization frequently conducts surveys. We take "field surveys" where we ask a series of questions of all the local hospitals in our system, asking for feedback on the hospital's performance, on the work of CEOs, and about their governing boards. We even ask for feedback on the performance of our corporate office.

Effective leaders of all sorts of organizations do similar things among their own constituency. Seeking out input and criticism helps breed an atmosphere of open communication. You don't want your people feeling hesitant to talk to you about their concerns. You don't want them wondering how honestly they can answer your questions, or worrying about how you might punish them for some critique. When you seek out input and criticism and receive it in a positive and nonretributive spirit, you send the message that you do care about people's thoughts and concerns, just as you value your organization's mission.

> *A Reality Conversation pushes people to see problems in the fundamental way they do business.*

And when you do seek out such input and criticism, ask for specifics. When I worked as a hospital administrator, physicians often came into my office to bend my ear and let me know they felt unhappy about something. Often, these doctors at first seemed reluctant to get into specifics.

I've never put a lot of weight on general criticism or input. When I talk to someone who expresses unhappiness with me or with something I've done (or haven't done), I want to know *exactly* how I made this person feel so unhappy and what I can do to improve the situation. Without that specific information, I can offer only platitudes, such as "I'll try to do better" . . . whatever *that* means. In the end, nothing gets resolved.

A leader must go the extra mile and let people know they can speak freely and specifically about their concerns. When my coworkers approach me to talk about some problem, I do everything I can to put that person at ease so that he or she can move beyond the superficial (generalities) and get down to what really concerns him or her (specifics). If I don't do that, I end up with little or no idea about what I can do to address the concern.

Don't ask anyone to do anything that you would not do yourself.

Overcoming Insecurities

Max DePree, the American businessman and author, once wrote, "The first responsibility of a leader is to define reality. The last is to say thank you. In between, the leader is a servant." That has always been one of my favorite quotations concerning leadership, and one I try to apply in my own life as a leader.

I feel especially drawn to the idea that my first responsibility as a leader is to define reality for the people who work under me. I understand how vitally important it is for me to define reality, especially that I clearly and purposefully let people know what I expect of them and what they should expect from me.

And what does defining reality have to do with responding well to criticism? Plenty! If you as a leader can't respond to criticism in a healthy way, then you will fail at your most important task. You will find it impossible to convey and define reality for the people who work for you. How can you define reality for others when you refuse to do it for yourself?

Insecurity is death to a leader's ability to lead effectively. An insecure leader will often do one of two things when facing criticism, neither of which will do any good for the organization.

Insecure Leader No. 1 has such a difficult time taking criticism that she covers herself in a thick, leathery skin that nothing can penetrate. Whether or not she means to, this leader communicates that she doesn't care about other people or what they think. After all, it's easier to demand that people blindly obey commands than to endure what feels like a personal attack.

Insecure Leader No. 2 takes "people pleasing" to a fault. Some past leaders in our system, even a few who worked in high positions, couldn't cut it in the long run simply because they tried to please everyone, all the time. Such leaders often wavered or demonstrated significant inconsistency in implementing our mission and vision statements. And who suffers? We all do.

No one can lead consistently who also tries to please everyone, all the time. This inconsistency leads to a lack of trust among the people who work under you. Eventually, they'll wonder whether they can trust anything you say.

Strategies for Overcomers

All of us harbor our own insecurities and fears. Those insecurities and fears can conspire to scuttle your efforts to lead and respond to criticism effectively. How can you learn to overcome them and become the kind of leader your organization needs?

Leaders may sit at the top, but that doesn't mean they have to go it alone. Consider a few strategies I've learned over the years to address my own insecurities and fears.

1. Look to your spouse/family.

Have you ever gone through a day, or maybe a string of days, where it seemed that no one spoke anything but critical words to you? Even when those who offer the criticisms care about you and your mission, it still can feel draining and deflating. On days like these, you can often find comfort and encouragement by leaning on your family, especially on your spouse and children (if you have them).

Even when you've endured the worst day you can imagine, even when you don't quite know how to respond to the arrows of criticism sticking out of your hide, you can normally find love, comfort, and encouragement at home. No one knows you better than the members of your own family, and someone at home might have some helpful pearls of wisdom to offer.

2. Reach out to a personal friend.

If you have a good friend from outside your work world—and

I hope you have *at least* one—you might find real help in talking with him or her about your work difficulties. Your friend may not know the specifics of your situation and may not even know much about your profession, but he knows you and might be able to help you see things from a different, more helpful perspective. It's amazing how a friend can sometimes consider your words and then offer the kind of encouragement or advice that can come only from those who see your situation from the outside.

3. Talk with a professional associate.

A professional associate—whether a fellow leader or CEO, a board chairman, or someone who does work similar to your own—can bring a perspective that sheds remarkable new light on your challenges. We encourage our leaders to utilize one another in this way, something of a "buddy system" in which people can act as sounding boards for each other.

Nothing can make an individual or a group more vulnerable than to work in a situation where the leadership has lost touch with reality.

I like to remind our leaders that they're not alone, even if they serve in some of our more rural locations. I want them to remember that they have a large, caring network of fellow leaders who stand willing and able to provide a listening ear and offer advice, support, and encouragement. I want the people in our organization to feel comfortable sharing their fears, insecurities, and concerns, so I remind them that they work among friends who share the same mission and the same corporate goals.

This support and encouragement can come in the form of a phone call or through conversation during a round of golf. Sometimes it involves sitting down with a more experienced executive, maybe someone in a superior position in the organization who understands on a personal level the fears and insecurities that come with leadership.

4. Lean on divine help.

According to the Gallup company, upward of 90 percent of people polled say they believe in God.[17] Since such a high percentage of people in the world (including myself) claim to believe in God, I feel I would be remiss if I don't address that fact. Now I realize not all readers of this book will consider themselves persons of faith, and that's okay. If personal faith is not something that describes you, I hope you don't take offense when I tell you that in my own life, I have found tremendous comfort, insight, and hope from relying on God's help.

> *Reality usually involves hard numbers and real-world data, so take the time to get that information and then lay it out as clearly as possible.*

If you are a leader and a person of faith, let me say that I believe one of the biggest mistakes leaders can make is to think they're on their own, as if God doesn't concern himself with their work. As the leader of a faith-based organization, I encourage my leaders to make sure they feel secure in their love relationship with God. When you feel secure in your relationship with God, then you find it much easier to get honest with him and with yourself about your insecurities and fears. We all feel insecure and fearful about *something.* We're human, after all. It's what you *do* with those negative feelings that makes all the difference.

Leaders run into serious problems when they are afraid to confess their fears. Honestly naming your insecurities to God will help you to overcome them. I also think asking for God's help is not a sign of leadership weakness, but rather a sign of honesty, humility, and openness. When I mentor young leaders, I even tell them to share their anger with God. He can handle it, and nothing surprises him. Get it out, seek divine wisdom, and allow it to strengthen your leadership.

Respond Well to Criticism

Remember the leader of the high-profile ministry who dismissed criticism with the words, "This is not me"? Even though he knew the criticisms had come from his own people, he blew them off, no doubt leaving his staff leaders wondering if he cared at all about them or what they thought.

Let me ask you, how do you think that man should have

responded? What could he have done to become the kind of leader his organization needed? What steps could he have taken to receive and process the criticism in a healthy way? How could he have begun the process of healing that needed to take place within his company?

I know how I *wish* the situation had played out. I can see it in my mind's eye:

> The leader stands up before his leadership staff. He knows the survey results, and he knows they came from the staff at large and not merely from a couple of malcontents. Rather than responding defensively or dismissively, he speaks to his leaders from the heart, with humility and even gratitude, for the courage to bring his weaknesses to his attention.
>
> "Look," he begins, "it's pretty clear to me that many of you—maybe all of you—have issues with my leadership and with how I handle certain situations within this company. I acknowledge that. I can see that I have certain weaknesses in how I lead, and those weaknesses have reached a level where they're hurting the organization and hurting many of you. I'm very sorry for that."
>
> Then this chastened leader talks to his leaders about some solutions to his problems.
>
> "I'm going to take this survey to our board of directors and talk to them about it. I'm also going to

share the results with someone I trust and ask what I can do to overcome my shortcomings and become the kind of leader you all deserve. I thank you for your support."

Assuming that this leader speaks sincerely and that his leadership staff truly believes in the mission of the organization, how do you think his people will respond?

Regardless how effective you may seem as a leader, how well you know your area of service, or how committed you are to your organization's mission, you will make mistakes from time to time. I certainly do. Of course, I try to live out the values I so passionately believe in. But when I slip up in some way, I know that some good people in our organization will bring my mistakes or bad decisions to my attention. If you are humble enough to listen when your people offer constructive criticism and resolute enough to make needed changes, then people can be incredibly forgiving. I've seen it time and again.

Without accountability an organization will either get stuck in a deep rut or implode.

We can never know how the people who work in such a dysfunctional work situation as the ministry described above might have responded if their leader had welcomed their criticisms with humility and contrition. But I'm willing to bet they would have offered him their forgiveness, support, and patience as he worked on himself to make the changes his organization required.

How Will You Respond?

While it's interesting to ponder how the leader mentioned above might have reacted better to the valid criticisms of his leadership, I can think of a much more useful question. How will *you* respond the next time you face intense criticism for something you've done or failed to do?

The ancient Scriptures give some great advice that I think applies here: "Everyone should be quick to listen, slow to speak and slow to become angry."[18] Let's take apart that advice, bit by bit.

Quick to listen: A good leader understands the importance of listening—especially to constructive criticism. All of us have "blind spots" and all of us make mistakes. But if we're wise, we listen when someone offers valid input or criticism.

Slow to speak: It has been said that it's better to keep your mouth shut and be thought a fool than to open your mouth and remove all doubt. It's all too human to respond to criticism with defensiveness. Most times, it's better just to listen patiently.

Slow to become angry: No one likes to get criticized, but a good leader knows better than to respond with anger. Rage breaks lines of communication and breeds further distrust and discontent.

So the next time you or your leadership gets criticized, don't get defensive or angry. Listen closely to the concerns being voiced. Ask clarifying questions. And then ask what you can do to perform better. And, as we stated at the beginning of this chapter, always put on the armor of your organization's mission.

In doing so, you will show yourself to be a strong, effective leader. And your people will love you for it.

14

Motivation Matters

Doing the Right Things for the Right Reasons

SMILING BACK A LITTLE GRIMLY AT THE hospital CEO sitting across from me, I leaned forward and asked, "Robert, what would you say if I were a banker?"

Robert (not his real name) gave me a blank stare.

I continued. "What if you were trying to borrow this money from a bank? What would you tell them about your future? How would you demonstrate this is a good investment? Because I have to tell you, one of a banker's first questions would be, 'Is this guy going to be back next month to just borrow more, and the next, and the next?'"

Robert's mouth opened. But no response came out. I could tell he didn't get why he should think in terms of talking to a banker. After all, wasn't this a *tax-exempt* organization involved in *service* to the community?

Robert had just given me a tour of his hospital, and I

had looked and listened carefully. They had plenty of medical technology to display and quite the full spectrum of departments. Robert wanted me to see all the healthcare they were giving the community, or at least all they were capable of giving.

But I knew this facility teetered in dangerous territory. In fact, I saw the wolf already crouching at the door; unless something changed, they'd go under. As director of a corporate network of hospitals to which Robert's facility belonged, I had to have what I call "The Reality Conversation."

When we sat down in Robert's office, I needed to put my cards on the table. Robert laid down his hand first, however. He had a request. Hospital CEOs usually do. He wanted to "invest" quite a bit of money to update his surgical facility. "I know we've got cash flow issues, having a hard time meeting payroll," he said, "but if we can just get some working capital from the corporation, that will really get us through."

That's when I asked him to think of me as a banker. And that's when he balked.

So I had to turn up the reality knob a bit. "I get the sense there's a bit of a dream state going on here. Folks keep assuming that the basic rules about finances, about keeping a business afloat, don't apply, that you'll just find a way to get more money, from *somewhere*."

Now Robert leaned back in his chair. I gave him a moment. Slowly he began nodding his head thoughtfully. I knew we had reached one of those critical points in our reality conversation. Which way would this CEO go?

Some people get too deeply invested in an unhealthy dependence on a parent organization or outside funding. They may nod their heads about the need for financial responsibility, but they can't shake their sense of a right to other people's money. They won't face reality unless you stop enabling them. Sometimes it's a pretty dramatic, painful stop.

Other people have responsible instincts but have fallen into bad habits. A reality conversation pushes them to see problems in the fundamentals, in the basic way they do business.

Fortunately, Robert proved to be the latter. He opened up about the financial challenges his hospital faced. He admitted how their revenue had slipped. And we began talking about ways to turn things around.

The requirement of facing reality sometimes slips by us, in the every-day busy-ness of managing. But defining reality comes down to this: Tell the truth, as clearly as you see it. Complete the following statements:

This is our purpose as an organization: ____________________.

This is the challenge we face: ____________________.

These are the objectives that top our list: ____________________.

These are the problems getting in our way: ____________________.

Nothing can make an individual or a group more vulnerable than to work in a situation where the leadership has lost touch with reality. But reality *will* strike, and probably sooner rather than later. If we don't prepare for it, our failure can cause untold pain, destroy our business, and put everyone who relies on us out of work.

When you define reality, you demonstrate that you care about people and that their future and well-being matters to you. Leaders who keep ignoring hard-to-face facts simply don't care enough. Leaders who keep putting off a confrontation with reality leave their people extremely vulnerable.

Defining reality means that you explain what's really happening in your community, your market, and your organization. You explain reality by laying out the facts. You make it clear, "This is what must happen if we are to reach our goals. If we fail to attain this and that, then these are the consequences."

Speaking the truth is about mission reality; it's about business reality; it's about cultural reality. Whatever your status as a leader, start there. *Facing reality is your vital first step in leadership.*

Reality usually involves hard numbers and real-world data. Take the time to get that information and then lay it out as clearly as possible. If you have a 1 percent profit margin and yet think you need to spend a lot of capital, get a grip on reality and admit that such a plan won't square. If your costs are way out of line, explain the dire situation to your associates and paint a stark picture of where this road will take you. But then paint

No one can lead consistently who also tries to please everyone, all the time.

another picture utilizing good benchmarking data that shows how your type of organization can do far better. Appeal to concrete, believable data.

Not everyone, of course, will believe you. People tend to attack data that delivers news they don't like. But continue to lay out the facts; make everyone face reality. In some cases, you may want to take your key associates on a tour of other organizations that do it right. Let them see what needs to be done in real time. Very often, the personal revelation, "Oh, that's how they do it," will lead to the conviction, "We can do that too!"

> *I don't knowingly let any of my leaders go into battle for a single day without the armor of our organization's mission.*

But no one will come to such a realization unless you insist that they focus on reality.

I realize this is a special challenge in tax-exempt organizations. Too many humanitarians, philanthropists, and people of faith fall into the trap of pretending they don't have to function in the real world. But of course, that's the only world where we all currently reside. We have to function in the real world. And so one of my passions is to make sure that the ideals of service survive and thrive *in the real world.*

To create reality for the people who report to you, you must consistently lay down the facts—in your conversations, in your reports, in your meetings. It all needs to jibe.

And remember that reality touches *all* of reality. Many managers try to avoid problems or conflicts, for example, by fudging on performance reviews. But that doesn't help anyone. Yes, you want to give people full credit for their accomplishments, but you also need to clearly confront subpar performance, because the reality is that substandard performance hurts the organization. Facing reality means that you look at *everything.*

If you want to build a healthy organizational culture, you need managers with good people skills—skills that don't gravitate to one extreme or the other. For example, some managers carry a harsh edge when they talk about something that needs work, or they sound demeaning when they discuss performance. Others have the opposite problem. They loathe confronting anyone; they shrink from directly saying anything that hints of conflict. They want everyone's approval so badly that they find it hard to deliver anything but good news. And so they step around problems or try to disguise them.

In either case, reality doesn't care. Eventually it will barge into the situation and blow it to pieces. Fairy tales are fun fiction, but they tend to blast organizations apart.

Suppose for a moment that you know of some managers in your organization who suffer from either of the maladies described above. What do you suppose happens, over time, when you fail to challenge such behavior? Do you think it just goes away? It doesn't. The only thing that goes away is trust. Why should an employee trust the person who puts her down or speaks offensively to her? Why should an employee trust the person who won't tell him what's really going on?

Never forget that employees talk to each other. What you say spreads quickly. A boss whose anger issues run over his people skills will leave a trail of hurt feelings. People learn quickly not to trust that boss with anything with even the remotest possibility of coming back to bite them.

And what about the people-pleasing boss who says one thing to this employee, and a very different thing to the next? Employees compare notes.

"Is this what she said to you?"

"No, why? Is that what she said to *you*?"

Trust cannot thrive in a dysfunctional environment, and no organization can thrive without trust. One of the best things you can do to build trust in your organization is to become known as a person who tells the truth. Determine to become a friend of reality, if you're not one already. Look it squarely in the face and help your colleagues to do the same. And don't wait. Reality certainly won't.

You Serve Them

A recent trend in publishing is books on the topic of "servant leadership." I just went to Amazon and looked up the term and got over five thousand results. Near the top of the list I saw books from Robert K. Greenleaf, Larry C. Spears, Stephen R. Covey, James C. Hunter, Ken Blanchard, James A. Autry, Bill B. Flint, John C. Maxwell, and many more. They speak of things like "legitimate power and greatness," of "the true essence of leadership," and even of "Building the Company Every Person Dreams of Working For and Every President Has a Vision Of Leading."

Who wouldn't want to work in an organization like that?

Please don't mistake my comment for sarcasm. In fact, I believe wholeheartedly in trying to live out the principle of servant leadership. I smile only at the subtle implication that this idea is something new and revolutionary. Revolutionary? Certainly. But new? Certainly not.

My own Boss said a long, long time ago that he "did not come to be served, but to serve."[19] He also said, "You call me 'Teacher' and 'Lord,' and rightly so, for that is what I am."[20] Boss, Teacher, and Servant—not a bad example for those of us called to lead.

> *Servant leaders take great pleasure in watching the growth, development, and success of those who report to them.*

While I don't claim to have anything like the ultimate take on servant leadership, I have learned several things about it over the years. Allow me to briefly outline four of the most important lessons I've gained.

1. No one is more important than anyone else.

Leaders of an organization have no more fundamental worth than any other person in the organization. Titles do not convey intrinsic human value. And I have found that people either believe that, or they don't.

Do *you* believe it?

If you really want to know the answer, ask yourself a simple question. When you walk down the hall, do you smile and greet only the people you see as important, those who have organizational weight? Or do you smile and greet everyone, most of the time?

Here's another question: Do you constantly make people "below" you wait? Do they have to sit for a while outside your office? If so, you're sending a signal that your time is more valuable than anybody else's time. But everyone has exactly the same amount of time. Time is precious; it's life ticking away. That's why I try to make sure people don't have to wait for me. I want my associates to know that I consider their time to be just as important as mine.

Insecurity is death to a leader's ability to lead effectively.

One simple way to accomplish this and to send a subtle message is to start meetings on time. I don't start early, unless everybody's already arrived. And I *never* start late. I don't wait on the "important people."

Let's say you're seated around a conference table, staring at six faces, but you're expecting eight. Sitting there and waiting for the other two to show up tells those six that the other two are more important.

I've known individuals who communicated a certain

attitude. They tell me that they have a full plate and so they may be late for a meeting, but I should wait until they get there. They discover very quickly that I don't wait. I don't put a meeting on hold just for them.

Yes, I get the occasional protest, and nearly always from people on the "high end." They have complained, "You started with this really important topic. I wanted to hear about it, and now I've missed it!"

I have a simple reply: "If you really want to hear about it, then get here on time. I do this because I don't want to communicate a message to anyone that your time is more important than anybody else's." I also explain that such a message would demean the contributions of others, because they would not see themselves as part of a team of equals.

Time and acknowledging others are two equalizing factors, but I would encourage you to find other simple ways of communicating to your team that no one is more important than anyone else.

2. Stay positive

A vital part of being a servant leader is helping your people to focus on the positive. Servant leaders take great pleasure in watching the growth, development, and success of those who report to them. *That's* what motivates good leaders. And from personal experience, I can tell you that after decades of seeking to become this kind of leader, it feels wonderfully fulfilling.

What's more, helping people to succeed by focusing

on the positive is the greatest single guarantor of my own success. After all, what will happen to me if everybody around me grows weak and fails? *I'm* going to fail. And far more importantly, the organization will fail.

Many managers today struggle right here because, whether in subtle or overt ways, they get extremely competitive with those who report to them. Such a competitive environment rarely stays positive. I work to combat such a scenario by focusing on one important objective: within a fairly short period of time, those who report to me will develop good, cohesive teamwork. So I tell my people both what I have to do and what they need to do in order for us to reach our goals together.

Servant leaders who keep things positive tend to see a lot more success than those who don't. The only real question is, do you want to succeed?

3. Become predictable.

I believe leaders best serve their people when they become predictable. Nothing lowers tension as much as predictability. This has become an important goal of mine. In fact, when I first take on some new role, I often tell my new coworkers, "Within three or four months, I believe you'll be able to predict, with 95 percent accuracy, my decision on most any question. You'll come to me when issues arise and you need a decision. But I believe you'll already know my response."

I have seen how uncomfortable employees tend to become when a manager makes decisions inconsistently. A leader without discernible, dependable principles that inform his or her decision making creates a lot of stress.

Help your people to learn, relatively quickly, why you make certain choices and why you take certain paths. Explain your governing principles well enough so that they can articulate those principles to others.

I suppose some leaders might resent overhearing a comment such as, "This is what he's going to say and this is why he's going to say it." But in fact, such predictability allows your people to function in a relaxed environment. It settles them down and makes them feel secure. Then they can go out and conduct their work without constantly looking over their shoulders or trying to cover their backsides (just in case).

> *Do the very best you know how—the very best—and then keep doing so until the end.*

Frankly, becoming predictable as a leader does not differ much from becoming a predictable parent. If your kids come to understand the basic rules of your home and the principles behind them, then likely you'll have a fairly harmonious family. If those principles make sense and you apply them consistently, then your kids will have a much happier childhood. And they'll be much less likely to play games with Mom and Dad, trying to exploit their unpredictability.

Predictability *matters.* And it matters all the more when an organization goes through changes or must deal with significant challenges. Even then, your guiding principles shine through and give people a reliable framework in which to function. You can say, "We're facing a new reality, but this is how we function. Although our goals may change, the most important things in this organization do not change."

Your consistency makes life so much easier for everyone. It makes people happy. No employee likes having to create some coherence in a job situation because the leader is all over the map. Unpredictability produces a highly stressful workplace that eventually burns out all but the most desperate employees.

So make your coworkers happy. And smile when they say, "You're really predictable, do you know that?"

4. Don't ask anyone to do anything you would not do yourself. Most of us can quickly spot a self-promoter. Managers motivated by personal aggrandizement, who give orders to make themselves look good, or who take credit for what others have done earn a soiled reputation that, sooner or later, trips them up.

If my people understand that I will never ask them to do anything that I wouldn't do myself, or that I won't ask them to work harder than I work, then they become much more likely to work hard at a thankless task. When I see my people overburdened with stress, I try to jump in and lend a hand. I'll empty a wastebasket or clean up an accident in the hall. People quickly figure out if a leader asks them to do certain things for the right reasons.

Are you making these demands to make yourself look good? Or are you making them because you want patients in this unit to receive Mother Teresa–level care? If they know you'll roll up your sleeves with the best of them, then you're much more likely to get at their heart strings. This is true not only for hospitals, but in every business—including yours.

Sometimes, however, you'll blow it. Your team also knows *that* when they see it, and some of the brave ones will tell you about it. And frankly, this can hurt. I know, because it happens to me every once in a while. I get worked up about something, I fail to react like a servant leader, and as a result, I get some push back. As I think about the encounter, however, I finally admit, "Hmmm. I need to make my own little personal course correction here."

> *When someone is displeased, I want to know exactly how I made this person feel so unhappy and what I can do to improve the situation.*

Servant leaders make mistakes, like everyone else. The successful ones learn to make exactly the same kinds of course corrections that they demand of others.

Tell Them "Thank You"

Years ago I left my role as a chief academic officer of a Baptist college and went to work for a fast-growing company that did research projects on a bid-out basis. It was hiring scientists and engineers like mad, but since scientists are a peculiar breed, the company soon discovered that the ones it had hired lacked any clue about how to manage people. They hired me because they hoped I could teach their managers how to deal with actual humans. But since we were growing so fast, they expected me to pull this off on the side.

I came up with the idea of holding an extended series of "brown bag lunches." Although I managed the chemistry division, managers from many other divisions also attended. Since I wanted some sort of core text to use as a base for our discussions, I picked Max DePree's potent little book, *Leadership Is an Art*. I'm sure it resonated with me because Max has a strong Christian world- view that clearly informs his perspective on leadership and management. His book examines the practical side of leadership, with chapter titles such as "Communicate!" and "Tribal Storytelling" and "Roving Leadership." But because I worked in a proudly secular, hard-working, hard-partying organization, I had to be careful about how I led our lunchtime discussions.

One of the biggest mistakes leaders can make is to think they're on their own, as if God doesn't concern himself with their work.

Even so, I went about living my life as I always had. I didn't smoke and didn't curse and treated women with respect, and as far as I knew, I was the only nondrinker in the whole place. Nobody gave me too hard of a time about it, though, and people seemed to enjoy and benefit from the lunches. Our chemistry division became quite profitable and, over time, the other divisions also enjoyed increasing success.

By the time I left the company, a good cross-section of colleagues in my division wrote me many wonderful notes of thanks, collected them all in a notebook, and then presented it to me. Decades later, I still keep that notebook in my office. Although I had carefully refrained from discussing my own Christian convictions, many of my coworkers expressed a great appreciation for both my convictions and my behavior. It felt humbling to me and even stunning to hear many of my colleagues say they felt a real sadness over my departure. Many of them thanked me for protecting them from the worst elements of the company's culture, which they saw as toxic and even a bit scary.

Yes, good leaders learn how to say "thank you." That's one of their chief responsibilities as leaders. But sometimes, when they're very, very lucky, those expressions of thanks come back to them in droves. I will always deeply cherish the notes of gratitude that I've received from appreciative employees and thankful coworkers who have expressed some genuine sadness to see me leave when my time at the helm had come to an end.

So to all of you I've worked with in the past, and to all of you who have taken the time to read this book, I say a heartfelt, "Thank you!"

Section Summary

Ten Insights about Outstanding Leadership

1. Leadership isn't for the weak of heart or for the thin-skinned. If you sit in the leader's chair, count on it, you will make some people angry.

2. The first responsibility of leaders is to define reality for the people who work under them, which cannot happen unless the leader learns to respond to criticism in a healthy way.

3. If you want to survive criticism and even use it for your benefit, then learn to approach it in the context of your organization's mission. Get a rock solid understanding of your mission, then practice explaining how your decisions enable your organization to further it.

4. Nothing can make an individual or a group more vulnerable than to work in a situation where the leadership has lost touch with reality. Reality usually involves hard numbers and real-world data. Take the time to get that information and lay it out as clearly as possible.

5. Sometimes your practice of relentless stewardship will require you to make decisions that certain people in your organization may not like very much. This is when you need to wear your organizations mission like armor. I don't knowingly let any of my leaders go into battle for a single day without the armor of our organization's mission.

6. Be humble. Remember, leaders of an organization have no more fundamental worth than any other person in the company.

7. Be predictable and consistent in how you live your company's mission, vision, and values. Nothing lowers tension like predictability.

8. Good leaders learn how to say "thank you." And they do it often.

9. One of the biggest mistakes leaders can make is to think they're on their own, as if God doesn't concern himself with their work.

10. Asking for God's help is not a sign of leadership weakness, but rather a sign of honesty, humility, and openness.

Acknowledgments

First, I must say that there would not be a book such as this on leadership had it not been for the dream of Todd Chobotar and his relentless determination that we were going to collaborate and produce a manuscript.

The original idea for this book came from Todd and he first had to talk me into it, then convince me that material for a manuscript could be obtained in ways other than having me sit down at a computer for long hours of writing—which I felt I didn't have. The initial material came through a recorded series of brown bag lunch talks I gave to young leaders on various management and leadership topics. The talks were followed by open question and answer sessions, also recorded. Then, in a most remarkable process, Todd conducted a series of recorded interviews with me. There were many interviews that took place over a fairly lengthy period of time, but as Todd asked probing questions I was constantly amazed at how that process helped me to remember situations that illustrated the principles I had come to believe in. I will be forever grateful to Todd for the genesis of this work.

I'm tremendously thankful for those who gave so generously of their time and expertise to improve the content and clarity of this book. First, to Steve Halliday for his exceptional writing and insights on leadership. Second, to peer reviewers Mark Hertling, Karen Tilstra, Josef Ghosn, Shirley Freed, and Scott Morris. Their wisdom added incredible value to this project.

I also want to acknowledge the influence on my learning, thinking and development by Don Welch, Mardian Blair, and Tom Werner. They happen to be the three individuals who served as presidents of Adventist Health System before me, and all three have been very important to my life in healthcare. When I started this journey more than thirty years ago, Don Welch was the president of our system. Toward the end of his career he stepped back and was working as a hospital chief executive in a division of the company for which I was then responsible. Don taught me the lesson of true humility and servant leadership as well as the importance of making sure the big strategic items were cared for in your leadership.

I worked for Mardian Blair for almost fifteen years, and I am so thankful for the opportunities he gave me along the way. Looking back, I'm amazed that he was willing to take a chance on someone without traditional experience and training in healthcare leadership. Mardian was a perfect model of unswerving integrity and commitment to the mission of Adventist healthcare.

From my beginning in healthcare, Tom Werner and I were peers in many ways. Because of our experiences and our age, we became close friends, and one of the treasures of my time in Adventist Health System has been his friendship.

I have never known anyone who could get more things done through the power of friendship and interpersonal relationships than Tom.

Throughout my time in Adventist Health System, I've had the pleasure of working with many outstanding people. There are too many for me to mention everyone, but I must thank the ones I've worked with in more recent times. Specifically Rich Reiner, who worked with me in the Florida Division and as the CEO of the Multi-State Division; Lars Houmann, who now is the president of Florida Hospital and the Florida Division; Brian Paradis, who was my chief financial officer at Florida Hospital and the Florida Division; Brent Snyder, who worked with me in Tennessee, with the Multi-State Division, and currently as our chief information officer; and finally Terry Shaw, who is the system CFO and chief operations officer. Each of these individuals is uniquely talented and deserves so much credit for the progress that we have made, and all are deeply committed to the mission of Adventist healthcare. I've learned as much from them as they may have learned from me.

Throughout my leadership life, I've had many outstanding personal assistants, but I must especially thank Dori Bair, who has been my assistant for the past fifteen years. No one else would know all that she has done to ease my work life and to take care of so many things that go above and beyond the normal call of duty. She and her husband, Ted, have become dear friends.

I have been incredibly blessed by my family. My two daughters, Jill and Jana, inspire me. They are so dedicated to the profession of teaching that they purposely carry on in a public school in Texas that serves young children from disadvantaged families. Their commitment to these children is so moving and effective that each has been selected as *Teacher of the Year* in their area. Jill and Jana are following in the steps of my mother, who was a teacher, and I only wish she could have lived to see the great work they are doing.

I am grateful for my grandchildren, Garrett, Gavin, and Hartlea. They have grown to become such outstanding young people in their values, outlook on life, and commitments. They make me proud every day.

And to Sharon, my dear, dear wife. You are the rock of my life, my best friend, and the one who knows me best. You help me see myself as I really am and have helped me grow through the years in countless ways. Those who know you, see you as an extraordinary professional musician and passionate teacher. I believe, you have accomplished more significant and important things than I ever have. I am so proud of you. In this life, you are my greatest blessing and treasure.

About The Author

DON JERNIGAN, PhD, serves as president and CEO of Adventist Health System—the largest Protestant not-for-profit healthcare system in the United States. With net revenue of more than $7 billion, Adventist Health System's 79,000 employees and nearly 9,000 affiliated physicians touch the lives of more than four million patients each year. The system's 44 hospitals are found in 10 states.

Dr. Jernigan's leadership journey has taken him to presidencies of three hospitals, including Florida Hospital—the largest admitting hospital in America. In the field of higher education, he served as a professor, department chair, vice president for academic affairs and executive vice president. Dr. Jernigan also served on active duty as an officer in the United States Navy. He received his Doctor of Philosophy degree in physical chemistry from Baylor University.

Jernigan is a Diplomate of the American College of Healthcare Executives. He is a member of the Board of Trustees for the Sanford-Burnham Medical Research Institute. He is a member of Sigma Xi, the Scientific Research Society, and is past chairman of the Economic Development Commission and a member of the Governor's Council. He has been a board member of the United Way, a senior citizens planning commission, several chambers of commerce, an industrial development foundation, and he has been active in Rotary International.

Dr. Jernigan is a sought-out speaker with a range of leadership knowledge in for-profit and not-for-profit companies as well as broad experience in the fields of healthcare, science, education, and the military. His leadership philosophy focuses on the importance of building trust, stewarding resources, and fulfilling mission.

Dr. Jernigan makes his home in Orlando, Florida. His personal hobbies and interests include photography, world history, U.S. presidents, and political science.

Notes

1 Bill George, *Authentic Leadership* (San Francisco: Jossey Bass, 2003), 62, 62.

2 Ibid., 70.

3 A theory from the world of communication studies has generated a treasure trove of insightful ideas for helping business leaders and others to successfully navigate the roiling waters of organizational vision change. Symbolic Convergence Theory (SCT) provides both theoretical and practical direction for those who seek assistance in helping their organizations embrace a new or modified vision. For an example of how one successful business employed the theory, see Cragan, John F., & Shields, Donald C. (1992). "The Use of Symbolic Convergence Theory in Corporate Strategic Planning: A Case Study." *Journal of Applied Communication Research* 20, no. 2, 199–218.

4 Anne Marie Bell. "Inspiring organizational change at Reuters." *Strategic Communication Management* 9, no. 5 (Aug/Sep 2005): 18–22.

5 Ann Zieger, *fiercehealthfinance.com*, December 24, 2008.

6 Alex Nixon, *Pittsburgh Tribune-Review* at *triblive.com*, April 26, 2013.

7 Michael Wyland, *nonprofitquarterly.com*, February 12, 2013.

8 Reuters, April 25, 2013.

9 It never feels good to fire someone or ask them to leave your company, but again: The mission is bigger than any individual. At a critical time in his ministry, even Jesus told a follower to leave (John 13:27–31).

10 *Kingman Daily Miner*, October 5, 1978.

11 www.Savemolives.com, www.wrac.com, www.mlive.com.

12 www.Corevalueslist.com.

13 June 30, 2009, www.michigan.gov/mdot.

14 For the full context of the story, see Deuteronomy 6, especially verses 6–8.

15 From *Six Months at the White House with Abraham Lincoln*, by Francis Bicknell Carpenter (Carlisle, MA: Applewood Books, 2008).

16 Words of Jesus from Luke 6:37, NCV.

17 According to a Gallup poll, 9 in 10 Americans say they believe in God. That number has varied only slightly since the Gallup organization first asked the question in the 1940s. Website accessed on June 30, 2013: http://www.gallup.com/poll/147887/americans-continue-believe-god.aspx.

18 Quotation from James 1:19.

19 Words of Jesus as quoted in Mark 10:45.

20 Words of Jesus as quoted in John 13:13.

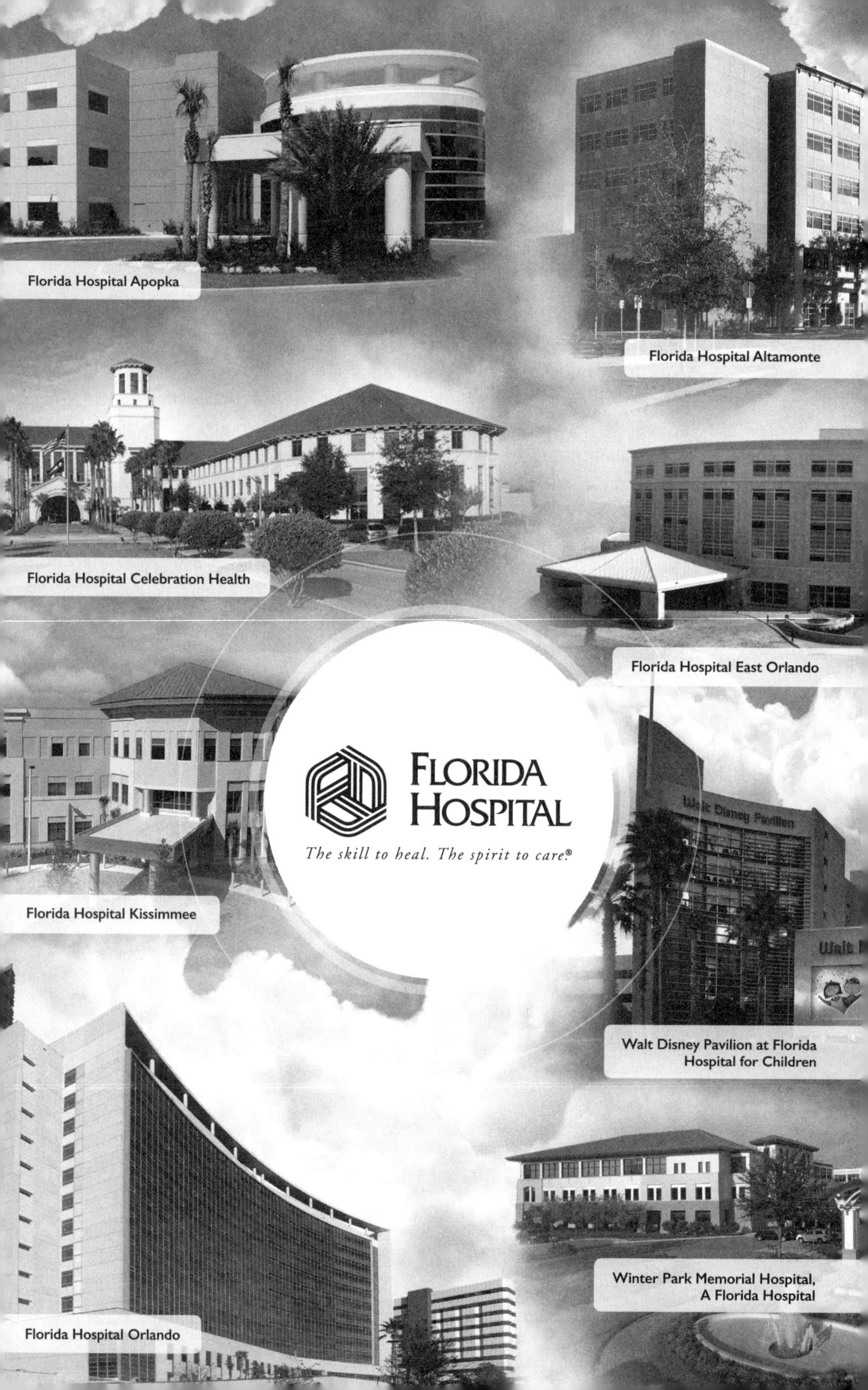

Florida Hospital Apopka

Florida Hospital Altamonte

Florida Hospital Celebration Health

Florida Hospital East Orlando

Florida Hospital Kissimmee

Walt Disney Pavilion at Florida Hospital for Children

Winter Park Memorial Hospital, A Florida Hospital

Florida Hospital Orlando

ABOUT FLORIDA HOSPITAL

For over one hundred years the mission of Florida Hospital has been: To extend the healing ministry of Christ. Opened in 1908, Florida Hospital is comprised of eight hospital campuses housing over 2,400 beds and twenty-two walk-in medical centers. With over 19,000 employees—including 2,200 doctors and 6,600 nurses—Florida Hospital serves the residents and guests of Orlando, the No. 1 tourist destination in the world. Florida Hospital has over 1.7 million patient visits a year. Florida Hospital is a Christian, faith-based hospital that believes in providing Whole Person Care to all patients—mind, body, and spirit. Hospital fast facts include:

LARGEST ADMITTING HOSPITAL IN AMERICA.

Ranked No. 1 in the nation for inpatient admissions by the American Hospital Association.

AMERICA'S HEART HOSPITAL.

Ranked No. 1 in the nation for number of heart procedures performed each year, averaging 22,000 cases annually. MSNBC named Florida Hospital "America's Heart Hospital" for being the No. 1 hospital fighting America's No. 1 killer—heart disease.

HOSPITAL OF THE FUTURE.

At the turn of the century, the Wall Street Journal *named Florida Hospital the "Hospital of the Future".*

ONE OF AMERICA'S BEST HOSPITALS.

Recognized by U.S. News & World Report *as "One of America's Best Hospitals" for ten years. Clinical specialties recognized have included: Cardiology, Orthopaedics, Neurology & Neurosurgery, Urology, Gynecology, Digestive Disorders, Hormonal Disorders, Kidney Disease, Ear, Nose & Throat and Endocrinology.*

LEADER IN SENIOR CARE.

Florida Hospital serves the largest number of seniors in America through Medicare with a goal for each patient to experience a "Century of Health" by living to a healthy hundred.

TOP BIRTHING CENTER.

Fit Pregnancy magazine named Florida Hospital one of the "Top 10 Best Places in the Country to have a Baby". As a result, The Discovery Health Channel struck a three-year production deal with Florida Hospital to host a live broadcast called "Birth Day Live." Florida Hospital annually delivers over 10,000 babies.

CORPORATE ALLIANCES.

Florida Hospital maintains corporate alliance relationships with a select group of Fortune 500 companies including Disney, Nike, Johnson & Johnson, Philips, AGFA, and Stryker.

DISNEY PARTNERSHIP.

Florida Hospital is the Central Florida health & wellness resource of the Walt Disney World® Resort. Florida Hospital also partnered with Disney to build the ground breaking health and wellness facility called Florida Hospital Celebration Health located in Disney's town of Celebration, Florida. Disney and Florida Hospital recently partnered to build a new state-of-the-art Children's Hospital.

HOSPITAL OF THE 21ST CENTURY.

Florida Hospital Celebration Health was awarded the Premier Patient Services Innovator Award as "The Model for Healthcare Delivery in the 21st Century".

SPORTS EXPERTS.

Florida Hospital is the official hospital of the Orlando Magic NBA basketball team. In addition, Florida Hospital has an enduring track record of providing exclusive medical care to many sports organizations. These organizations have included: Disney's Wide World of Sports, Walt Disney World's Marathon Weekend, the Capital One Bowl, and University of Central Florida Athletics. Florida Hospital has also provided comprehensive healthcare services for the World Cup and Olympics.

CONSUMER CHOICE AWARD WINNER.

Florida Hospital has received the Consumer Choice Award from the National Research Corporation every year from 1996 to the present.

PUBLICATIONS.

Florida Hospital Publishing can help you live life to the fullest with a variety of health and wellness books and other resources uniquely focused on Whole Person Health.

Visit: www.FloridaHospitalPublishing.com

FLORIDA HOSPITAL

601 E. Rollins Street, Orlando, FL 32803

FloridaHospital.org | 407-303-5600

GUIDES AND ASSESSMENTS

Pregnancy Guides
Expert advice on how to be CREATION Healthy while expecting.

Senior Guide
Share the CREATION Health principles with seniors and help them be healthier and happier as they live life to the fullest.

Self-Assessment
This instrument raises awareness about how CREATION Healthy a person is in each of the eight major areas of wellness.

Pocket Guide
A tool for keeping people committed to living all of the CREATION Health principles daily.

Tote Bag
A convenient way for bringing CREATION Health materials to and from class.

Tumbler
Practice good Nutrition and keep yourself hydrated with a CREATION Health tumbler in an assortment of fun colors.

MARKETING MATERIALS

Postcards, Posters, Stationery, and more
You can effectively advertise and generate community excitement about your CREATION Health seminar with a wide range of available marketing materials such as enticing postcards, flyers, posters, and more.

Bible Stories
God is interested in our physical, mental, and spiritual well-being. Throughout the Bible you can discover the eight principles for full life.

CREATION HEALTH BOOKS

CREATION Health Discovery
Written by Des Cummings Jr., PhD, Monica Reed, MD, and Todd Chobotar, this wonderful companion resource introduces people to the CREATION Health philosophy and lifestyle.

CREATION Health Devotional
In this devotional you will discover stories about experiencing God's grace in the tough times, God's delight in triumphant times, and God's presence in peaceful times.

English: Hardcover
Spanish: Softcover

CREATION HEALTH RESOURCES

The Love Fight (Softcover)

Are you going to fight for love or against each other? In *The Love Fight*, Drs. Tony Ferretti and Peter Weiss address a new dichotomy: the clash between Achievers and Connectors. The authors illustrate how this common encounter can create a mutually satisfying relationship. Their expertise will walk you through the scrimmage between those who want to accomplish and those who want to relate.

Pain Free For Life (Hardcover)

In *Pain Free For Life*, Scott C. Brady, MD,—founder of Florida Hospital's Brady Institute for Health—shares for the first time with the general public his dramatically successful solution for chronic back pain, fibromyalgia, chronic headaches, irritable bowel syndrome, and other "impossible to cure" pains. Dr. Brady leads pain-racked readers to a pain-free life using powerful mind-body-spirit strategies used at the Brady Institute—where more than 80 percent of his chronic-pain patients have achieved 80–100 percent pain relief within weeks.

If Today Is All I Have (Softcover)

At its heart, Linda's captivating account chronicles the struggle to reconcile her three dreams of experiencing life as a "normal woman" with the tough realities of her medical condition. Her journey is punctuated with insights that are at times humorous, painful, provocative, and life-affirming.

SuperSized Kids (Hardcover)

In *SuperSized Kids*, Walt Larimore, MD, and Sherri Flynt, MPH, RD, LD, show how the mushrooming childhood obesity epidemic is destroying children's lives, draining family resources, and pushing America dangerously close to a total healthcare collapse—while also explaining, step by step, how parents can work to avert the coming crisis by taking control of the weight challenges facing every member of their family.

SuperFit Family Challenge – Leader's Guide

Perfect for your community, church, small group, or other settings.

The SuperFit Family Challenge Leader's Guide Includes:

- Eight weeks of pre-designed PowerPoint™ presentations.
- Professionally designed marketing materials and group handouts from direct mailers to reading guides.
- Training directly from Author Sherri Flynt, MPH, RD, LD, across six audio CDs.
- Media coverage and FAQ on DVD.

CREATION HEALTH RESOURCES

Forgive To Live (English: Hardcover / Spanish: Softcover)

In *Forgive to Live* Dr. Tibbits presents the scientifically proven steps for forgiveness—taken from the first clinical study of its kind conducted by Stanford University and Florida Hospital.

Forgive To Live Workbook (Softcover)

This interactive guide will show you how to forgive – insight by insight, step by step—in a workable plan that can effectively reduce your anger, improve your health, and put you in charge of your life again, no matter how deep your hurts.

Forgive To Live Devotional (Hardcover)

In his powerful new devotional, Dr. Dick Tibbits reveals the secret to forgiveness. This compassionate devotional is a stirring look at the true meaning of forgiveness. Each of the fifty-six spiritual insights includes motivational Scripture, an inspirational prayer, and two thought-provoking questions. The insights are designed to encourage your journey as you begin to *Forgive to Live*.

Forgive To Live God's Way, A Small Group Resource (Softcover)

Forgiveness is so important that our very lives depend on it. Churches teach us that we should forgive, but how do you actually learn to forgive? In this spiritual workbook, noted author, psychologist, and ordained minister Dr. Dick Tibbits takes you step-by-step through an eight-week forgiveness format that is easy to understand and follow.

Forgive To Live Leader's Guide

Perfect for your community, church, small group, or other settings.

The Forgive To Live Leader's Guide Includes:

- Eight weeks of pre-designed PowerPoint™ presentations.
- Professionally designed customizable marketing materials and group handouts on CD-Rom.
- Training directly from author of *Forgive to Live* Dr. Dick Tibbits across six audio CDs.
- Media coverage DVD.
- CD-Rom containing all files in digital format for easy home or professional printing.
- A copy of the first study of its kind conducted by Stanford University and Florida Hospital showing a link between decreased blood pressure and forgiveness.

Leadership in the Crucible of Work (Hardcover)

What is the first and most important work of a leader? (The answer may surprise you.) In *Leadership in the Crucible of Work*, noted speaker, poet, and college president Dr. Sandy Shugart takes readers on an unforgettable journey to the heart of what it means to become an authentic leader.

CREATION Health Breakthrough (Hardcover)

Blending science and lifestyle recommendations, Monica Reed, MD, prescribes eight essentials that will help reverse harmful health habits and prevent disease. Discover how intentional choices, rest, environment, activity, trust, relationships, outlook, and nutrition can put a person on the road to wellness. Features a three-day total body rejuvenation therapy and four-phase life transformation plan.

CREATION Health Devotional for Women (English)

Written for women by women, the *CREATION Health Devotional for Women* is based on the principles of whole-person wellness represented in CREATION Health. Spirits will be lifted and lives rejuvenated by the message of each unique chapter. This book is ideal for women's prayer groups, to give as a gift, or just to buy for your own edification and encouragement.

A Desk Reference to Personalizing Patient Care (Hardcover)

Aurora Realin, MBA, CDM, discusses how diversity is increasing at a rapid pace. Clinicians committed to providing the best patient care must become familiar with the key attitudes and expectations of patients whose culture, religious beliefs, generation, or level of disability differs from their own.

Now there is help. *Personalizing Patient Care* is a valuable guide for improving a caregiver's understanding of how a patient's background may affect their needs, preferences, and expectations related to the delivery of care.